Leviticus & Romans

Read the Bible Again for the First Time

Echoes Bible

Volume III

2025

World English Bible (WEB)

Echoesbible.com

Leviticus & Romans
Read the Bible Again for the First Time
Echoes Bible, Volume III, 2025

The Echoes Bible Foundation is a non-profit Christian ministry dedicated to the discovery, dissemination, education and application of literary connections between the inspired books of the Bible. It is organized as a U.S. based 501(c)3.

Echoes Bible Foundation
13359 North Highway 183
Suite 406-679
Austin, Texas 78750
publish@echoesbible.org

Paul, the Apostle to the Gentiles, first acknowledged Jesus as the Messiah as a result of encountering him on the road to Damascus. Prior to that he had been known as Saul, a learned leader among the Pharisee sect of Judaism in 1st century Judea, a student of the revered rabbi Gamaliel. His thinking and imagination had been shaped by deep acquaintance with the Torah, Wisdom Literature, and Prophets (Tanakh), what Christians in the modern age generally call "the Old Testament." How, exactly, did his biblically shaped mind and soul guide his composition of his letters? The quotations from scripture are clear enough, but in ten years of study, we have discovered in the text echoes of the Old Testament structure, theme, and vocabulary in Paul's letters. In this volume, we will explore those echoes between the book of Leviticus and the Epistle to the Romans.

Dedication:
To Paul the Apostle

ISBN Paperback: 978-1-970720-04-4
Cover Design by Stephen Douglas Alexander, Layout by Echoes Bible Foundation

1. Christianity. 2 Bibles. 3. Bible Commentary. 4. Bible Study. 5. Old Testament. 6. New Testament.
I. Echoes Bible Foundation
II. Leviticus & Romans. Read the Bible Again for the First Time. Echoes Bible. Volume III. 2025.

INTRODUCTION

Upon receiving the revelation from God on the road to Damascus, Paul's entire world was turned upside down. A zealous student of the Torah, having studied under Gamaliel (Acts 22:3), Paul would then spend about three years in Arabia and Damascus before going up to Jerusalem to meet Peter and James (Gal. 1:18–19). His time in Arabia must have included extended periods of revisiting the Torah, seeking to understand how he could have missed the work of Christ Jesus within it. How fascinating it would have been to sit beside Paul, to converse with him, as he began reading the Torah anew in the light of Christ. In Arabia, Paul would have started to perceive how Christ was inextricably present in every book, every story, every paragraph, and perhaps even every verse that he had studied so intently for so many years. Given God's call to him on the road to Damascus (Acts 26:17), Paul must also have re-read the Torah with an eye toward discerning God's plan to bring the Gentiles into a saving knowledge of Jesus Christ.

When Paul was set apart for ministry, he experienced the joy of sharing the Gospel directly with both Jew and Gentile. After establishing assemblies in various locations, he would then write letters to them. The New Testament preserves more than a dozen of these letters, now recognized as the inspired Word of God. Paul wrote in Greek, and when quoting the Old Testament, he necessarily did so in Greek as well, and his direct quotations are numerous. At times he also addressed topics by appealing to principle rather than direct quotation. With great conviction he affirms that "every Scripture is inspired by God and profitable for teaching, for reproof, for correction, and for training in righteousness" (2 Tim. 3:16). Yet Paul is not an easy writer to understand. Peter himself acknowledges this in 2 Peter 3:16, observing that Paul's writings contain elements that are difficult to grasp and therefore more susceptible to being twisted.

The document you hold in your hand is likely unlike any other Bible you have encountered. The Echoes Bible Foundation asserts that this approach to reading the Scriptures is more firmly grounded than ever, for it provides additional insight into how—and from where—Paul formulated his words, anchoring his approach directly back to the inspired Word of God itself. This work enables the reader to study the books of Leviticus and Romans side by side, section by section, and to see firsthand from where part of Paul's inspiration was drawn.

Our claim is that Paul used the book of Leviticus as his primary outline when addressing the church at Rome. Both books are counted among the most complex in all of Scripture: Leviticus, with its intricate and detailed treatment of the processes and purposes of the feasts and offerings; and Romans, with its equally intricate and detailed exposition of salvation through Jesus Christ.

The following table shows a sampling of some of the echoes in Leviticus and how they inspired some of Paul's verses.

Leviticus	Romans
1 & 2 Pleasant aroma	1 First uses of "Spirit"
3 Two kidneys	1 Salvation for both Jew and Greek
6 Law of burnt offering & law of meal offering	2 Sinned under the law => Judged by the law
8 Urim and Thummim on the high priest's breastplate	3 The Jews were trusted with the revelations/oracles of God
8 Moses: Blood on Aaron's and sons' ears	3 There is no one righteous; no not one
9 Wave offering to Yahweh	3 Law of works? No, a law of faith
12 Plague of Leprosy	5 Through one "trespass" all were condemned
14 Cleansed Leper: 2 birds, 1 killed and 1 set free	6 We died to sin? How could we live in it longer?
17 Strangers who live as sojourners among them	8 Spirit of adoption by whom we cry Abba Father!
22 To be accepted, offer a male without defect from the bulls, sheep or goats	12 Be transformed... so you may prove what is the good, well-pleasing and perfect will of God.
23 It is a Sabbath to Yahweh in all your dwellings	13 Put on the Lord Jesus Christ and make no provision for the flesh and all its lusts
27 A female valued at 30 shekels	16 Receive Phoebe in a way worthy of the saints
27 These are the commandments which Yahweh commanded	16 My Good News and preaching of Jesus Christ according to the revelation of the mystery

This document divides Leviticus and Romans into 114 *sectional pairings*, each consisting of connections between one or more verses from the two books. Because Leviticus contains more verses than Romans, a greater number of verses from Leviticus are, on average, paired with fewer verses from Romans. These **pairings** are presented in a side-by-side format so that the reader may discern what in Leviticus may have partially inspired Paul in writing his corresponding words to the Romans. Within each **pairing**, we have also identified what we believe to be more specific connections between particular statements in Leviticus and the words of Paul. We refer to these more specific, individual connections as *echoes*, and in this document we have identified more than 400 echoes.

For example, in Leviticus 1:1, the opening phrase "Yahweh called to Moses" contains the word **called**, which is paired with the word **called** in Romans 1:1, where Paul describes himself as "called to be an apostle." This constitutes the first echo. Next, the phrase **Tent of Meeting**—the place where Moses went in from among the people to meet directly with God—is paired with the phrase **set apart** in Romans 1:1, as part of the expression "set apart for the Good News of God." This constitutes the second echo. The use of **bold-underline** does not suggest that the second echo is more significant than the first; it serves merely as a visual aid to help the reader quickly identify the corresponding echoes. At times, non-bold underlining is also used.

In this initial sectional pairing, a total of two echoes are identified. These identified echoes are not necessarily the only echoes present, but in a black-and-white print format we have intentionally limited our selection to echoes that appear in sequential order. For example, in a sectional pairing containing six echoes, the first bolded echo in Leviticus will always and only be paired with the first bolded phrase in Romans, and so forth through the entire section. Notes appear after many pairings to explain less obvious echoes and any exceptions in format.

The *Echoes Bible* employs the World English Bible (WEB) translation, as it is available without copyright restrictions. At the same time, we often select echoes with careful attention to the Hebrew and Greek underlying the English words, and we frequently highlight such insights in the notes. That being said, the reader is encouraged to view the identified echoes as suggested connections between two inspired texts. While our suggestions themselves are not necessarily inspired, we firmly believe that the sheer preponderance, the richness of meaning, and the poetic beauty of these echoes will, in their totality, deepen a reader's love for God's Word, heighten their awe of God, and perhaps even carry them back to the joy of their first encounter with salvation—allowing them to *read the Bible again for the first time.*

The connections between these two books are real and we believe, intentional. The inspired text of Leviticus, helping to awaken Paul's vast knowledge of scripture in many other passages, overshadowed by the living work of the Holy Spirit, has resulted in the God-breathed inspired words of Romans that we read today. Because the Word of God is inspired, we have every expectation that the Holy Spirit can speak to the reader through the Echoes Bible and reveal the truth of God's intentions in the words written by Paul.

Our vision is not that any new truth would emerge from these pairings, but rather that the echoes would further demonstrate how Paul's words are firmly anchored in the truth of all Scripture, thereby greatly reducing the potential for errors in interpretation. In agreement with Peter's warning, we likewise desire that Paul's words will no longer be twisted by "ignorant or unsettled persons."

The Echoes Bible Editing Team

Leviticus 1	Romans 1

Lev 1:1 Yahweh **called** to Moses, and spoke to him from the Tent of Meeting, saying, **2** "Speak to the children of Israel, and tell them, 'When any **man of you offers an offering** to Yahweh, you shall offer your offering of the livestock, from the herd, and from the flock.	**Rom 1:1** Paul, a servant of Jesus Christ, **called** to be an apostle, **set apart** for the Good News of God,

NOTE: [Vayikra.] *Vayikra* (Hebrew name for Leviticus) is divided into ten Jewish Torah portions (Parshat), the first matching the book's name. The Echoes Bible's sections align with these boundaries and are marked with brackets in the notes.

Lev 1:3 "'If his **offering is a burnt offering** from the herd, <u>he shall offer a male without defect</u>. He shall offer it at the door of the Tent of Meeting, that he may be accepted before Yahweh. **4** He shall lay his hand on the head of the burnt offering, and it shall be accepted for him to make atonement for him. **5** He shall kill the bull before Yahweh. Aaron's **sons**, the priests, shall present the blood and sprinkle the blood around on the altar that is at the door of the Tent of Meeting. **6** He shall <u>skin</u> the burnt offering and cut it into pieces.	**Rom 1:2** which he **promised** before through his prophets in the holy Scriptures, **3** <u>concerning his Son</u>, who was born of the **offspring** of David according to the <u>flesh</u>,

Lev 1:7 The sons of Aaron the priest shall put fire on the altar and lay wood in order on the fire; **8** and Aaron's sons, the priests, shall lay the pieces, the head, and the fat in order on the wood that is on the fire which is on the altar; **9** but its innards and its legs he shall wash with water. The priest shall burn all of it on the altar, for a burnt offering, an offering made by fire, of a **pleasant aroma to Yahweh**. **Lev 10** "'If his offering is from the flock, from the sheep or from the goats, for a burnt offering, he shall offer a male without defect. **11** He shall <u>kill it on the north side</u> of the **altar before Yahweh**. Aaron's sons, the priests, shall sprinkle its blood around on the altar. **12** He shall cut it into its pieces, with its head and its fat. The priest shall lay them in order on the wood that is on the fire which is on the altar, **13** but the innards and the legs he shall wash with water. The priest shall offer the whole and burn it on the altar. It is a burnt offering, an offering made by fire, of a pleasant aroma to Yahweh.	**Rom 1:4** who was declared to be the Son of God with power, according to the **Spirit of holiness**, by the resurrection from the <u>dead</u>, **Jesus Christ our Lord**,

NOTE: Regarding the echo "kill it on the north side," Jesus was crucified outside the city walls on the north side of the city.

Lev 1:14 "'If his offering to Yahweh is a burnt offering of birds, then he shall offer his offering from **turtledoves or of young pigeons**. 15 The priest shall bring it to the altar, and wring off its head, and burn it on the altar; and its blood shall be drained out on the side of the altar; 16 and he shall take away its crop and its feathers and cast it beside the altar on the east part, in the place of the ashes. 17 He shall tear it by its wings but **shall not divide it apart**. The priest shall burn it on the altar, on the wood that is on the fire. It is a burnt offering, an offering made by fire, of a pleasant aroma to **Yahweh**.

Rom 1:5 through whom we received grace and apostleship for obedience of **faith among all the nations** for his name's sake; 6 among whom you are also called **to belong to Jesus Christ**; 7 to all who are in Rome, beloved of God, called to be saints: Grace to you and peace from God our Father and the **Lord Jesus Christ**.

NOTE: The echo of turtledoves and young pigeons is proposed to echo "faith among all the nations" because when Jesus was presented to the Lord in Jerusalem after his birth with "a pair of turtledoves or two young pigeons," Simeon immediately prophesied that salvation was coming to the gentiles. (Luke 2:22-32).

Leviticus 2   Romans 1:8

Lev 2:1 "'When **anyone offers an offering of a meal offering to Yahweh**, his offering shall be of fine flour. He shall pour oil on it and put frankincense on it. 2 He shall bring it to Aaron's sons, the priests. He shall take his handful of its fine flour, and of its oil, with all its frankincense, and the priest shall burn its memorial on the altar, an offering made by fire, of a **pleasant aroma** to **Yahweh**. 3 That which is left of the meal offering shall be Aaron's and his sons'. It is a most holy thing of the **offerings** of Yahweh made by fire.

Rom 1:8 First, **I thank my God through Jesus Christ** for all of you, that your faith is proclaimed throughout the whole world. 9 For God is my witness, whom I serve in my **spirit** in the Good News of his **Son**, how unceasingly I make mention of you always in my **prayers**,

NOTE: Thanks to God is a kind of offering (Psalm 50:14), and so is prayer (Ps. 141:2).

Lev 2:4 "'When you offer an offering of a meal offering baked in the oven, it shall be unleavened cakes of fine flour mixed with oil, or unleavened wafers anointed with oil. **5** If your offering is a meal offering made on a griddle, it shall be of unleavened fine flour, mixed with oil. **6** You shall cut it in pieces and pour oil on it. It is a meal offering. **7** If your offering is a meal offering of the pan, it shall be made of fine flour with oil. **8** You shall bring the meal offering that is made of these things to Yahweh. It shall be presented to the priest, and he shall bring it to the altar. **9** The priest shall take from the meal offering its memorial, and shall burn it on the altar, an offering made by fire, of a pleasant aroma to Yahweh. **10** <u>That which is left of the meal offering shall be Aaron's and his sons'</u>. It is a **most holy thing of the offerings** of Yahweh made by fire.

Rom 1:10 requesting, if by any means now at last I may be prospered by the will of God to come to you. **11** For I long to see you, that I may impart to you some spiritual gift, to the end that you may be established; **12** that is, **<u>that I with you may be encouraged in you</u>**, each of us **by the other's faith**, both yours and mine.

NOTE: Faith is required to believe that when the meal offerings are eaten together with the sons, that they are a most holy thing.

Lev 2:11 "'No meal offering which you shall offer to Yahweh shall be made with yeast; for you shall burn no yeast, nor any honey, as an offering made by fire to Yahweh. **12** As an offering of <u>**first fruits**</u> you shall offer them to Yahweh, but they shall not rise up as a pleasant aroma on the altar. **13** Every offering of your meal offering you shall season with salt. You shall not allow the salt of the covenant of your God to be lacking from your meal offering. With all your offerings you shall offer salt.

14 "'If you offer a meal offering of first fruits to Yahweh, you shall offer for the meal offering of your first fruits fresh heads of grain parched with fire, crushed new grain. **15** You shall put oil on it and lay frankincense on it. It is a meal offering. **16** The priest shall **burn as its memorial part of its crushed grain and part of its oil, along with all its frankincense**. It is an offering made by fire to Yahweh.

Rom 1:13 Now I don't desire to have you unaware, brothers, that I often planned to come to you, and was hindered so far, **<u>that I might have some fruit</u>** among you also, even as among the rest of the Gentiles. **14** I am debtor both to Greeks and to foreigners, both to the wise and to the foolish. **15** So as much as is in me, I am eager to **preach the Good News** to you also who are in Rome.

NOTE: Frankincense is a component of the meal offering (Leviticus 2:1) and was offered to Christ as a gift (Matthew 2:11), who is the very essence of the Good News preached by Paul.

Leviticus 3	Romans 1:16
Lev 3:1 "'If his offering is a sacrifice of **peace offerings**; if he offers it from the herd, whether male or female, he shall offer it without defect before <u>Yahweh</u>. **2** He shall lay his hand on the head of his offering and kill it at the door of the Tent of Meeting. Aaron's sons, the priests, shall sprinkle the blood around on the altar. **3 He shall offer of the sacrifice of peace offerings an offering made by fire to Yahweh**. The fat that covers the innards, and all the fat that is on the innards, **4 and the two kidneys**, and the fat that is on them, which is by the loins, and the cover on the liver, with the kidneys, he shall take away. **5** Aaron's sons shall burn it on the altar on the burnt offering, which is on the wood that is on the fire: it is an offering made by fire, of a pleasant aroma to Yahweh. **6** "'If his offering for a **sacrifice of peace offerings** to Yahweh is from the flock, male or female, he shall offer it without defect. **7** If he offers a lamb for his offering, then he shall offer it before Yahweh; **8** and he shall lay his hand on the head of his offering and kill it before the Tent of Meeting. Aaron's sons shall sprinkle its blood around on the altar. **9** Of the **sacrifice of peace offerings** he shall offer an offering made by fire to Yahweh: its fat, the entire tail fat, he shall take away close to the backbone; and the fat that covers the innards, and all the fat that is on the innards, **10** and the two kidneys, and the fat that is on them, which is by the loins, and the cover on the liver, with the kidneys, he shall take away. **11** The priest shall burn it on the altar: it is the food of the offering made by fire to Yahweh.	**Rom 1:16** For I am not ashamed of the **Good News** of <u>Christ</u>, because it is the **power of God for salvation** for everyone who believes, for the **Jew first, and also for the Greek**. **17** For in it is revealed God's righteousness from **faith** to <u>faith</u>. As it is written, "But the righteous shall live by faith."

NOTE: The two kidneys function independently, but the body is much stronger when both are working. God's plan is for Jew and Greek to both thrive to together to bring the full expression of Christ's body on the earth.

Lev 3:12 "'<u>**If his offering is a goat**</u>, then he shall offer it before Yahweh. **13** He shall lay his hand on its head and kill it before the Tent of Meeting; and the sons of Aaron shall sprinkle its blood around on the altar. **14** Of it he shall offer his offering, an offering made by fire to Yahweh: the fat that covers the innards, and all the fat that is on the innards, **15** and the two kidneys, and the fat that is on them, which is by the loins, and the cover on the liver, with the kidneys, he shall take away. **16** The priest shall burn them on the altar: it is the food of the offering made by fire, for a **pleasant aroma**; all the fat is Yahweh's. **17** "'It shall be a <u>**perpetual statute**</u> throughout your generations in all your dwellings, that you shall eat neither fat nor blood.'"

Rom 1:18 <u>**For the wrath of God is revealed**</u> from heaven against all ungodliness and unrighteousness of men who suppress the truth in unrighteousness, **19** because that which is known of God is revealed in them, for God revealed it to them. **20** For **the invisible things of him** since the creation of the world are clearly seen, being perceived through the things that are made, even his <u>**everlasting power**</u> and divinity, that they may be without excuse.

NOTE: The connection of a goat to the wrath or judgement of God may be found in Matthew 25:32. An aroma is present and real, but invisible.

Leviticus 4   Rom. 1:21

Lev 4:1 Yahweh spoke to Moses, saying, **2** "Speak to the children of Israel, saying, 'If anyone **sins unintentionally**, in any of the things which Yahweh has commanded not to be done, and does any one of them, **3** if the anointed priest **sins so as to bring guilt** on the people, then let him offer for his sin which he has sinned a young bull without defect to Yahweh for a sin offering. **4** He shall bring the bull to the door of the Tent of Meeting before Yahweh; and he shall lay his hand on the head of the bull and kill the bull before Yahweh. **5** The anointed priest shall take some of the blood of the bull and bring it to the Tent of Meeting. **6** The priest shall dip his finger in the blood, and sprinkle some of the blood seven times before Yahweh, before the **veil** of the sanctuary. **7** The priest shall put some of the blood on the horns of the altar of sweet incense before Yahweh, which is in the Tent of Meeting; and he shall pour out the rest of the blood of the bull at the base of the altar of burnt offering, which is at the door of the Tent of Meeting.

Rom 1:21 Because knowing God, they **didn't glorify** him as God, and **didn't give thanks**, but became vain in their reasoning, and their senseless heart was **darkened**.

NOTE: Romans 1:21 begins the downward slide of sin with the word "didn't". Leviticus Ch. 4 introduces the concept of unintentional sin. While Leviticus speaks of God creating a *veil* to His holiness, Paul looks from another angle and suggests that sin creates a separation from God, like a veil over the human heart, *darkening* it from the knowledge of God.

Lev 4:8 He shall take all the fat of the bull of the sin offering from it: the fat that covers the innards, and all the fat that is on the innards, **9** and the two kidneys, and the fat that is on them, which is by the loins, and the cover on the liver, with the kidneys, he shall remove, **10** as it is removed from the bull of the sacrifice of peace offerings. The priest shall burn them on the altar of burnt offering. **11 The bull's skin, all its flesh, with its head, and with its legs, its innards, and its dung, 12** he shall carry the whole bull outside of the camp to a clean place, where the ashes are poured out, and burn it on wood with fire. It shall be burned where the ashes are poured out.

Rom 1:22 Professing themselves to be wise, they became fools, **23** and traded the glory of the incorruptible God for the likeness of an image of corruptible man, and of birds, and **four-footed animals**, and creeping things.

NOTE: Leviticus reveals how animals can be sacrificed to bring peace. Romans describes how the worship of those same animals brings foolishness and corruption. The ancient cultures of the Middle East and Mediterranean Basin revered the bull in its pagan mythology.

Lev 4:13 "'**If the whole congregation of Israel sins**, and **the thing is hidden from the eyes of the assembly**, and they have done any of the things which Yahweh has commanded not to be done, and are guilty; **14** when the sin in which they have sinned is known, then the assembly shall offer a young bull for a sin offering, and bring it before the Tent of Meeting. **15** The elders of the congregation shall lay their hands on the head of the bull before Yahweh; and the bull shall be killed before Yahweh. **16** The anointed priest shall **bring some of the blood of the bull** to the Tent of Meeting. **17** The priest shall dip his finger in the blood and sprinkle it seven times before Yahweh, before the veil. **18** He shall put some of the blood on the horns of the altar, which is before **Yahweh**, that is in the Tent of Meeting; and the rest of the blood he shall pour out at the base of the altar of burnt offering, which is at the door of the Tent of Meeting. **19** All its fat he shall take from it and burn it on the altar. **20** He shall do this with the bull; as he did with the bull of the sin offering, so he shall do with this; and the priest shall make atonement for them, and they shall be forgiven. **21** He shall carry the bull outside the camp and burn it as he burned the first bull. It is the sin offering for the assembly.

Rom 1:24 Therefore God also **gave them up in the lusts of their hearts to uncleanness**, that their bodies should be dishonored among themselves; **25** who **exchanged the truth of God for a lie** and worshiped and **served the creature** rather than the **Creator**, who is blessed forever. Amen.

NOTE: When Paul wrote "served the creature" he may have been thinking about how a godly action such as "bringing the blood of the bull to the Tent of Meeting" can be easily twisted by the world into a focus on the bull (the creature) rather than a proper focus on God who created the bull.

Lev 4:22 "'When a ruler sins and unwittingly does **any one of all the things which Yahweh his God has commanded not to be done**, and is guilty, **23** if his **sin in which he has sinned** is made known to him, he shall bring as his offering a goat, a male without defect. **24** He shall lay his hand on the head of the goat and kill it in the place where they kill the burnt offering before Yahweh. It is a sin offering. **25** The priest shall take some of the blood of the sin offering with his finger and put it on the horns of the altar of burnt offering. He shall pour out the rest of its blood at the base of the altar of burnt offering. **26** All its fat he shall burn on the altar, like the fat of the sacrifice of peace offerings; and the priest shall make atonement for him concerning his sin, and he shall be forgiven.

Rom 1:26 For this reason, God gave them up **to vile passions**. For their women changed the natural function into that which is against nature. **27** Likewise also the men, leaving the natural function of the woman, burned in their lust toward one another, men **doing what is inappropriate with men**, and receiving in themselves the due penalty of their error.

Lev 4:27 "'If anyone of the common **people sins unwittingly**, in **doing any of the things which Yahweh has commanded not to be done,** and is guilty, **28** if his sin which he has sinned is made known to him, then he shall bring for his offering a goat, a female without defect, for his sin which he has sinned. **29** He shall lay his hand on the head of the sin offering and kill the sin offering in the place of burnt offering. **30** The priest shall take some of its blood with his finger and put it on the horns of the altar of burnt offering; and the rest of its blood he shall pour out at the base of the altar. **31** All its fat he shall take away, like the fat is taken away from the sacrifice of peace offerings; and the priest shall burn it on the altar for a pleasant aroma to Yahweh; and the priest shall make atonement for him, and he shall be forgiven.

32 "'If he brings a lamb as his offering for a sin offering, he shall bring a female without defect. **33** He shall lay his hand on the head of the sin offering and kill it for a sin offering in the place where they kill the burnt offering. **34** The priest shall take some of the blood of the sin offering with his finger and put it on the horns of the altar of burnt offering; and all the rest of its blood he shall pour out at the base of the altar. **35** He shall remove all its fat, like the fat of the lamb is removed from the sacrifice of peace offerings. The priest shall burn them on the altar, on the offerings of Yahweh made by fire. The priest shall make atonement for him concerning **his sin that he has sinned**, and he shall be forgiven.

Rom 1:28 Even as **they refused to have God in their knowledge**, God gave them up to a reprobate mind, **to do those things which are not fitting**; 29 being filled with all **unrighteousness**, sexual immorality, wickedness, covetousness, malice; full of envy, murder, strife, deceit, evil habits, secret slanderers, **30** backbiters, hateful to God, insolent, arrogant, boastful, inventors of evil things, disobedient to parents, **31** without understanding, covenant breakers, without natural affection, unforgiving, unmerciful;

NOTE: Paul is not letting the world rest in an excuse that they were just sinning unintentionally. His echo includes the word "refused." Perhaps an echo may be heard from his words in the other direction, from Romans towards the Leviticus passage. Could Paul be suggesting that the person in Leviticus who "sins unwittingly" was doing so because he was refusing to become more knowledgeable of God's commands? Concerning Rom. 1:29, the echo of "unrighteousness," indeed the echo of the entire list of sins, may be found in Lev. 4:35, which foreshadows that though a coming priest (Jesus Christ) a path to forgiveness may be found for even the most heinous of sins.

Leviticus 5   Rom. 1:32

Lev 5:1 "'If anyone sins, in that he hears a public adjuration to testify, he being a witness, whether he has seen or known, if he doesn't report it, then he shall bear his iniquity. **2** "'Or if anyone touches any unclean thing, whether it is the carcass of an unclean animal, or the carcass of unclean livestock, or the carcass of unclean creeping things, and it is hidden from him, and he is unclean, then he shall be guilty. **3** "'Or if he touches the uncleanness of man, whatever his uncleanness is with which he is unclean, and it is hidden from him; when he knows of it, then he shall be guilty. **4** "'Or if anyone swears rashly with his lips to do evil or to do good—whatever it is that a man might utter rashly with an oath, and it is hidden from him; **when he knows of it, then he will be guilty of one of these. 5 It shall be, when he is guilty of one of these, he shall confess that in which he has sinned; 6 and he shall bring his trespass offering to Yahweh for his sin which he has sinned**: a female from the flock, a lamb or a goat, for a sin offering; and the priest shall make atonement for him concerning his sin.

Rom 1:32 who, <u>knowing the ordinance of God, that those who practice such things are worthy of death, not only do the same, but also approve of those</u> who practice them.

NOTE: In Romans 1:32, the end of the downward slide of sins has now been reached. The echo in Leviticus "when he knows of it" and "shall confess" correctly declares that atonement is not possible without both knowledge and confession of sin.

Leviticus 5:7   Romans 2

Lev 5:7 "'If he can't afford a lamb, then he shall bring his trespass offering for that in which he has sinned, two turtledoves, or two young pigeons, to Yahweh; one for a sin offering, and the other for a burnt offering. **8** He shall bring them to the priest, who shall first offer that which is for the sin offering. He shall wring off its head from its neck but shall not sever it completely. **9** He shall sprinkle some of the blood of the sin offering on the side of the altar; and the rest of the blood shall be drained out at the base of the altar. It is a sin offering. **10** He shall offer the second for a burnt offering, according to the ordinance; and the priest shall make atonement for him concerning his sin which he has sinned, and he shall be forgiven.

11 "'But if he can't afford two turtledoves or two young pigeons, then he shall bring as his offering for that in which he has sinned, one tenth of an ephah of fine flour for a sin offering. He shall put no oil on it, and he shall not put any frankincense on it, for it is a sin offering. **12** He shall bring it to the priest, and the priest shall take his handful of it as the memorial portion, and burn it on the altar, on the offerings of Yahweh made by fire. It is a sin offering. **13** The priest shall make atonement for him concerning **his sin that he has sinned in any of these things**, and he shall be forgiven; and the rest shall be the priest's, as the meal offering.'"

Rom 2:1 Therefore you are without excuse, O man, whoever you are who judge. For in that which you judge another, you condemn yourself. For you who judge practice the same things. **2** We know that the judgment of God is according to truth against those who practice such things. **3** Do you think this, O man who judges those who practice such things, **and do the same**, that you will escape the judgment of God?

NOTE: In Leviticus 5:7, the extent of one's offering may be reduced if one's resources are lacking, but no person is *excused* from their responsibility before God.

Lev 5:14 Yahweh spoke to Moses, saying, **15** "If anyone commits a trespass, and sins unwittingly regarding Yahweh's holy things, then he shall bring his trespass offering to Yahweh: a ram without defect from the flock, according to your estimation in **silver by shekels**, according to the shekel of the sanctuary, for a trespass offering. **16** He shall make restitution for that which he has sinned in the holy thing, and shall add a fifth part to it, and give it to the priest; and the priest shall make atonement for him with the ram of the trespass offering, and he shall be forgiven.

17 "If anyone sins, doing any of the things which Yahweh has commanded not to be done, though he didn't know it, he is still guilty, and shall bear his iniquity. **18 He shall bring a ram without defect from of the flock**, according to your estimation, for a trespass offering, to the priest; **and the priest shall make atonement for him concerning the thing in which he sinned and didn't know it, and he shall be forgiven**. **19** It is a trespass offering. He is certainly guilty before Yahweh."

Rom 2:4 Or do you despise the **riches** of his goodness, forbearance, and patience, not knowing that the **goodness of God** leads you to **repentance**?

NOTE: [Vayikra ends.] God provided a ram in the thicket for Abraham to sacrifice. That God used this event to both spare Isaac as well as to show his goodness that would lead the entire world to repentance.

Leviticus 6	Romans 2:5
Lev 6:1 Yahweh spoke to Moses, saying, **2** "If anyone sins, and commits a trespass against Yahweh, and deals falsely with his neighbor in a matter of deposit, or of bargain, or of robbery, or has oppressed his neighbor, **3** or has found that which was lost, and dealt falsely therein, and swearing to a lie—in any of these things that a man sins in his actions— **4** then it shall be, if he has **sinned, and is guilty**, he shall restore that which he took by robbery, or the thing which he has gotten by oppression, or the deposit which was committed to him, or the lost thing which he found, **5** or anything about which he has sworn falsely: **he shall restore it in full**, and shall add a fifth part more to it. To him to whom it belongs he shall give it, in the day of his being found guilty. **6** He shall bring his trespass offering to Yahweh: a ram without defect from the flock, according to your estimation, for a trespass offering, to the priest. **7** The **priest** shall make atonement for **him** before Yahweh, and he shall be forgiven concerning whatever he does to become guilty."	**Rom 2:5** But according to your hardness and unrepentant heart you are treasuring up for yourself wrath in the **day of wrath, revelation**, and of the righteous judgment of God, **6** who "will **pay back to everyone** according to their works:" **7** to those who by perseverance in well-doing seek for glory, honor, and incorruptibility, eternal life; **8** but to those who are self-seeking and don't obey the truth, but obey unrighteousness, will be wrath, indignation, **9** oppression, and anguish on every soul of man who does evil, to the **Jew** first, and also to the **Greek**. **10** But glory, honor, and peace go to every man who does good, to the Jew first, and also to the Greek. **11** For there is no partiality with God.

NOTE: [Tzav.] In Romans 2:9, the word "Jew" may be an echo of "priest" but if so, how is the word "Greek" an echo of "him"? The answer is found in Leviticus 6:1 which opens the passage with the phrase "if anyone sins." Paul sees in the word "anyone" the rest of the world, capturing this idea in the word "Greek" (e.g. Rom. 3:9-10,10:12).

Lev 6:8 Yahweh spoke to Moses, saying, **9** "Command Aaron and his sons, saying, 'This is the **law** of the burnt offering: the burnt offering shall be on the hearth on the altar all night until the morning; and the fire of the altar shall be kept burning on it. **10** The priest shall put on his linen garment, and he shall put on his linen trousers upon his body; and he shall remove the ashes from where the fire has consumed the burnt offering on the altar, and he shall put them beside the altar. **11** He shall take off his garments, and put on other garments, and carry the ashes outside the camp to a clean place. **12** The fire on the altar shall be kept burning on it, it shall not go out; and the priest shall burn wood on it every morning. He shall lay the burnt offering in order upon it and shall burn on it the fat of the peace offerings. **13** Fire shall be kept burning on the altar continually; it shall not go out.

14 "'This is the <u>law</u> of the meal offering: the sons of Aaron shall offer it before Yahweh, before the altar. **15** He shall take from there his handful of the fine flour of the meal offering, and of its oil, and all the frankincense which is on the meal offering and shall burn it on the altar for a pleasant aroma, as its memorial, to Yahweh. **16** That which is left of it Aaron and his sons shall eat. It shall be eaten without yeast in a holy place. They shall eat it in the court of the Tent of Meeting. **17** It shall not be baked with yeast. I have given it as their portion of my offerings made by fire. It is most holy, as the sin offering, and as the trespass offering. **18** Every male among the children of Aaron shall eat of it, as their portion forever throughout your generations, from the offerings of Yahweh made by fire. Whoever touches them shall be holy.'"

Rom 2:12 For as many as have sinned without the **law** will also perish without the law.

As many as have sinned under the **law** will be judged by the law.

Lev 6:19 Yahweh **spoke to Moses**, saying, **20** "This is the offering of Aaron and of his sons, which they shall offer to Yahweh in the day when he is anointed: the tenth part of an ephah of fine flour for a meal offering perpetually, half of it in the morning, and half of it in the evening. **21** <u>**It shall be made with oil in a griddle. When it is soaked, you shall bring it in**</u>. You shall offer the meal offering in baked pieces for a pleasant aroma to Yahweh. **22** The anointed priest that will be in his place from among his sons shall offer it. By a statute forever, it shall be wholly burned to Yahweh. **23** Every meal offering of a priest shall be wholly burned. It shall not be eaten."

Rom 2:13 For it isn't the **hearers of the law** who are righteous before God, but the **doers of the law** will be justified.

Lev 6:24 Yahweh spoke to Moses, saying, **25** "Speak to Aaron and to his sons, saying, 'This is the law of the sin offering: in the place where the burnt offering is killed, the sin offering shall be killed before Yahweh. It is most holy. **26** The priest who offers it for sin shall eat it. It shall be eaten in a holy place, in the **court** of the Tent of Meeting. **27** Whatever shall touch its flesh shall be holy. When there is any of its blood sprinkled on a garment, you shall wash that on which it was sprinkled in a holy place. **28** But the earthen vessel in which it is boiled shall be broken; and if it is boiled in a bronze vessel, it shall be scoured and rinsed in water. **29** Every male among the priests shall eat of it. It is most holy. **30** No sin offering, of which any of the blood is brought into the Tent of Meeting to make atonement in the Holy Place, shall be eaten. It shall be burned with fire.

Rom 2:14 (for when **Gentiles** who don't have the law do by nature the things of the law, these, not having the law, are a law to themselves, **15** in that they show the work of the law written in their hearts, their conscience testifying with them, and their thoughts among themselves accusing or else excusing them) **16** in the day when God will judge the secrets of men, according to my Good News, by Jesus Christ.

NOTE: The connection between the two sides of this pairing is a consciousness of sin. Those who bring a sin offering to the priest, have consciousness of sin and have been given a means of dealing with it. This same consciousness is at work in the Gentiles, having "the law written in their hearts." The word "court" is suggested to be the echo of "Gentiles" because of their use in Revelation 11:2.

Leviticus 7   Romans 2:17

Lev 7:1 "This is the law of the trespass offering. It is most holy. **2** In the place where they kill the burnt offering, he shall kill the trespass offering; and its blood he shall sprinkle around on the altar. **3** He shall offer all of its fat: the fat tail, and the fat that covers the innards, **4** and he shall take away the two kidneys, and the fat that is on them, which is by the loins, and the cover on the liver, with the kidneys; **5** and the **priest** shall burn them on the altar for an offering made by fire to Yahweh: it is a trespass offering. **6** Every male among the priests may eat of it. It shall be eaten in a holy place. **It is most holy**. **7** "'As is the sin offering, so is the trespass offering; there is one law for them. The priest who makes atonement with them shall have it. **8** **The priest who offers any man's burnt offering** shall have for himself the skin of the burnt offering which he has offered. **9** Every meal offering that is baked in the oven, and all that is prepared in the pan and on the griddle, shall be the priest's who offers it. **10** Every meal offering, mixed with oil or dry, belongs to all the sons of Aaron, one as well as another.

11 "'This is the law of the sacrifice of peace offerings, which one shall offer to Yahweh: **12** If he offers it for a thanksgiving, then he shall offer with the sacrifice of thanksgiving unleavened cakes mixed with oil, and unleavened wafers anointed with oil, and cakes mixed with oil. **13** He shall offer his offering with the sacrifice of his peace offerings for thanksgiving **with cakes of leavened bread**. **14** Of it he shall offer one out of each offering for a heave offering to **Yahweh**. It shall be the priest's who sprinkles the blood of the peace offerings.

Rom 2:17 Indeed you bear the name of a **Jew**, rest on the law, glory in God, **18** know his will, and approve **the things that are excellent**, being instructed out of the law, **19** and are confident that you yourself are a guide of the blind, **a light to those who are in darkness**, **20** a corrector of the foolish, a teacher of babies, having in the law the form of knowledge and of the truth. **21** You therefore who teach another, don't you teach yourself? You who preach that a man shouldn't steal, do you steal? **22** You who say a man shouldn't commit adultery; do you commit adultery? You who abhor idols, do you rob temples? **23** You who glory in the law, through your **disobedience of the law** do you dishonor God? **24** For "the **name of God** is blasphemed among the Gentiles because of you," just as it is written.

NOTE: The priest who "offers any man's burnt offering" should be "a light to those who are in darkness," but that light was indeed corrupted by Nadab and Abihu who offered strange fire before the Lord (Leviticus 10:1). Paul's phrase "disobedience to the law" is an interesting echo of "cakes of *leavened* bread" rather than *unleavened* bread. Paul may have been thinking about the connection of *leaven* to *malice and wickedness* (see 1 Corinthians 5:8) and chose this moment in his letter to challenge the Roman church's sin in an exceedingly strong way.

Lev 7:15 The **flesh of the sacrifice** of his peace offerings for thanksgiving shall be eaten on the day of his offering. He shall not leave any of it until the morning. **16** "'But if the sacrifice of his offering is a vow, or a freewill offering, it shall be eaten on the day that he offers his sacrifice. On the next day what remains of it shall be eaten, **17** but what remains of the flesh of the sacrifice on the third day shall be burned with fire. **18** If any of the <u>**flesh of the sacrifice of his peace offerings is eaten on the third day, it will not be accepted**</u>, and it shall not be credited to him who offers it. It will be an abomination, and the soul who eats any of it will bear his iniquity.

19 "'The flesh that touches any unclean thing shall not be eaten. It shall be burned with fire. As for the flesh, everyone who is clean may eat it; **20** but the soul who eats of the **flesh of the sacrifice of peace offerings that belongs to Yahweh, having his uncleanness on him, that soul shall be cut off from his people**. **21** When anyone touches any unclean thing, the uncleanness of man, or an unclean animal, or any unclean abomination, and eats some of the flesh of the sacrifice of peace offerings which belong to Yahweh, that soul shall be cut off from his people.'"

Rom 2:25 For **circumcision** indeed profits, if you are a doer of the law, but if you are a **transgressor of the law**, your **circumcision has become uncircumcision**.

NOTE: The echo of Leviticus 7:20 "cut off from his people" to "uncircumcision" is suggested because of their connection in Genesis 17:14.

Lev 7:22 Yahweh spoke to Moses, saying, **23** "Speak to the children of Israel, saying, 'You shall eat no fat, of bull, or sheep, or goat. **24** The fat of that which dies of itself, and the fat of that which is torn of animals, may be used for any other service, but you shall in no way eat of it. **25** For whoever eats the fat of the animal which men offer as an offering made by fire to Yahweh, even the soul who eats it shall be cut off from his people. **26 You shall not eat any blood, whether it is of bird or of animal, in any of your dwellings**. **27** <u>Whoever it is who eats any blood, that soul shall be cut off from his people</u>.'"

28 Yahweh spoke to Moses, saying, **29** "Speak to the children of Israel, saying, 'He who offers the sacrifice of his peace offerings to Yahweh shall bring his offering to Yahweh out of the sacrifice of his peace offerings. **30** With his own hands he shall bring the offerings of Yahweh made by fire. He shall bring the fat with the breast, that the breast may be waved for a wave offering before Yahweh. **31** The priest shall burn the fat on the altar, but the breast shall be Aaron's and his sons'. **32** The right thigh you shall give to the priest for a heave offering out of the sacrifices of your peace offerings. **33** He among the sons of Aaron who offers the blood of the peace offerings, and the fat, shall have the right thigh for a portion. **34** For the waved breast and the heaved thigh I have taken from the children of Israel out of the sacrifices of their peace offerings and have given them to Aaron the priest and to his sons as their portion forever from the children of Israel.'"

Rom 2:26 If therefore **the uncircumcised keep the ordinances of the law**, won't his uncircumcision be accounted as circumcision? **27** Won't the uncircumcision, which is by nature, if it fulfills the law, judge you, <u>**who with the letter and circumcision are a transgressor of the law**</u>? **28** For he is not a Jew who is one outwardly, neither is that circumcision which is outward in the flesh;

NOTE: Most cultures around the world generally abstain from eating blood. This fact could have inspired Paul in the first echo.

Lev 7:35 This is the consecrated portion of Aaron, and the consecrated portion of his sons, out of the offerings of Yahweh made by fire, in the day when he presented them to minister to Yahweh **in the priest's office**; **36** which Yahweh commanded to be given them of the children of Israel, in the day that he anointed them. It is their portion forever throughout their generations.

37 This is the law of the burnt offering, of the meal offering, of the sin offering, of the trespass offering, **of the consecration**, and of the sacrifice of peace offerings, **38** which Yahweh **commanded Moses in Mount Sinai**, in the day that he commanded the children of Israel to offer their offerings to <u>Yahweh</u>, in the wilderness of Sinai.

Rom 2:29 but **he is a Jew** who is one inwardly, and **circumcision is <u>that of the heart, in the spirit</u>**, not in the **letter**; whose praise is not from men, but from <u>God</u>.

NOTE: Circumcision is a form of consecration (Genesis 17:10-14).

Leviticus 8

Romans 3

Lev 8:1 Yahweh spoke to Moses, saying, **2** "Take **Aaron and his sons with him**, and the garments, and the anointing oil, and the bull of the sin offering, and the two rams, and the basket of unleavened bread; **3** and assemble all the congregation at the door of the Tent of Meeting." **4** Moses did as Yahweh commanded him; and the congregation was assembled at the door of the Tent of Meeting. **5** Moses said to the congregation, "This is the thing which Yahweh has commanded to be done."

6 Moses brought Aaron and his sons and washed them with water. **7** He put the tunic on him, tied the sash around him, clothed him with the robe, put the ephod on him, and he tied the skillfully woven band of the ephod on him and fastened it to him with it. **8 He placed the breastplate on him. He put the Urim and Thummim in the breastplate**. **9** He set the turban on his head. He set the golden plate, the holy crown, on the front of the turban, as Yahweh commanded Moses.

10 Moses took the anointing oil and anointed the tabernacle and all that was in it and sanctified them. **11** He sprinkled it on the altar seven times, and anointed the altar and all its vessels, and the basin and its base, to sanctify them. **12** He poured some of the anointing oil on Aaron's head, and anointed him, to sanctify him. **13** Moses brought Aaron's sons, and clothed them with tunics, and tied sashes around them, and put headbands on them, as Yahweh commanded Moses.

Rom 3:1 Then **what advantage does the Jew have**? Or what is the profit of circumcision? **2** Much in every way! Because first of all, **they were entrusted with the revelations of God**. **3** For what if some were without faith? Will their lack of faith nullify the faithfulness of God? **4** May it never be! Yes, let God be found true, but every man a liar. As it is written, "that you might be justified in your words, and might prevail when you come into judgment." **5** But if our unrighteousness commends the righteousness of God, what will we say? Is God unrighteous who inflicts wrath? (I speak like men do.) **6** May it never be! For then how will God judge the world? **7** For if the truth of God through my lie abounded to his glory, why am I also still judged as a sinner? **8** Why not (as we are slanderously reported, and as some affirm that we say), "Let's do evil, that good may come?" Those who say so are justly condemned.

NOTE: The word "revelations" in Romans 3:2 is *logion* (Greek) and is often translated "oracles." While the Bible is certainly considered to be the oracles of God, and the Jewish people were entrusted with preserving these scriptures, the Urim the Thummim in the breastplate of High Priest was a priestly device for obtaining "oracles" to obtain the will of God in specific situations for the king, the high court, or for someone serving the needs of the community. (For more, see the *Jewish Virtual Library*.)

Lev 8:14 He took the bull of the sin offering, and Aaron and his sons laid their hands on the head of the bull of the sin offering. **15** He killed it; and Moses took the blood and put it around on the horns of the altar with his finger, and purified the altar, and poured out the blood at the base of the altar, and sanctified it, to make atonement for it. **16** He took all the fat that was on the innards, and the cover of the liver, and the two kidneys, and their fat; and Moses burned it on the altar. **17** But the bull, and its skin, and its flesh, and its dung, he burned with fire outside the camp, as Yahweh commanded Moses.

18 He presented the ram of the burnt offering. Aaron and his sons laid their hands on the head of the ram. **19** He killed it; and Moses sprinkled the blood around on the altar. **20** He cut the ram into its pieces; and Moses burned the head, and the pieces, and the fat. **21** He washed the innards and the legs with water; and Moses burned the whole ram on the altar. It was a burnt offering for a pleasant aroma. It was an offering made by fire to Yahweh, as Yahweh commanded Moses.

22 He presented the other ram, the ram of consecration. Aaron and his sons laid their hands on the head of the ram. **23** He killed it; and Moses took some of its blood and put it on the tip of Aaron's right ear, and on the thumb of his right hand, and on the great toe of his right foot. **24** He brought Aaron's sons; **and Moses put some of the blood on the tip of their right ear, and on the thumb of their right hand, and on the great toe of their right foot**; and Moses sprinkled the **blood around on the altar**. **25** He took the fat, the fat tail, all the fat that was on the innards, the cover of the liver, the two kidneys and their fat, and the right thigh; **26** and out of the basket of unleavened bread that was before Yahweh, he took one unleavened cake, a cake of oiled bread, and one wafer, and placed them on the fat and on the right thigh. **27** He put all these in Aaron's hands and in his sons' hands and waved them for a wave offering before Yahweh. **28** Moses took them from their hands and burned them on the altar on the burnt offering. They were a consecration offering for a pleasant aroma. It was an offering made by fire to Yahweh. **29** Moses took the breast and waved it for a wave offering before Yahweh. It was Moses' portion of the ram of consecration, as Yahweh commanded Moses.

Rom 3:9 What then? **Are we better than they? No, in no way. For we previously warned both Jews and Greeks that they are all under sin**. **10** As it is written, "**There is no one righteous; no, not one**. **11** There is no one who understands. There is no one who seeks after God. **12** They have all turned away. They have together become unprofitable. There is no one who does good, no, not one." **13** "Their throat is an open tomb. With their tongues they have used deceit." "The poison of vipers is under their lips." **14** "Their mouth is full of cursing and bitterness."

NOTE: Moses put blood on the right ear, hand and great toe of the high priest, and his sons. Paul's words, "are we better than they" indicate that if the priesthood needed "the blood" foreshadowing the blood of Christ, then of course everyone else would need it as well.

Lev 8:30 Moses took some of the anointing oil, and some of the blood which was on the altar, and sprinkled it on Aaron, on his garments, and on his sons' garments with him, and sanctified Aaron, his garments, and his sons, and his sons' garments with him.

31 Moses said to Aaron and to his sons, "Boil the flesh at the door of the Tent of Meeting, and there eat it and the bread that is in the basket of consecration, as I commanded, saying, 'Aaron and his sons shall eat it.' **32** What remains of the flesh and of the bread you shall burn with fire. **33 You shall not go out from the door** of the Tent of Meeting for seven days, until the days of your consecration are fulfilled: for he shall consecrate you seven days. **34** As has been done today, so Yahweh has commanded to do, to make atonement for you. **35 At the door of the Tent of Meeting you shall stay day and night seven days, and keep Yahweh's command, that you don't die**: for so I am commanded." **36 Aaron and his sons did all the things which Yahweh commanded** by Moses.

Rom 3:15 Their feet are swift to shed blood. 16 Destruction and misery are in their ways. **17 The way of peace, they haven't known**." **18** "There is no **fear of God** before their eyes."

NOTE: [Tzav ends.] In Leviticus 8:35, the idea of staying put at the door of the Tent of Meeting, is contrasted in Romans 3:15 by those who do the opposite: both to leave the presence of God and then engage in sinful acts. The third phrase "fear of God" is embodied by the actions of Aaron and his sons in Lev. 8:36 who exhibited a holy fear of God by doing *all* the things which Yahweh commanded.

Leviticus 9	Romans 3:19

Lev 9:1 On the eighth day, **Moses called** Aaron and his **sons, and the elders** of Israel; **2** and he said to Aaron, "Take a calf from the herd for a sin offering, and a ram for a burnt offering, without defect, and offer them before Yahweh. **3** You shall speak to the children of Israel, saying, 'Take a male goat for a sin offering; and a calf and a lamb, both a year old, without defect, for a burnt offering; **4** and a bull and a ram for peace offerings, to sacrifice before Yahweh; and a meal offering mixed with oil: for today Yahweh appears to you.'" **5** They brought what Moses commanded before the Tent of Meeting. **All the congregation came near and stood before Yahweh**.

Rom 3:19 Now we know that whatever things **the law says**, it speaks to those who are under the law, that **every mouth** may be closed, and **all the world may be brought under the judgment of God**. **20** Because by the works of the law, no flesh will be justified in his sight; for through the law comes the knowledge of sin.

NOTE: [Shemini.] No person in the congregation, the eldership, or the priesthood did *not* need to make an offering for sin. In that sense, every mouth was closed.

Lev 9:6 Moses said, "This is the thing which Yahweh commanded that you should do; and Yahweh's glory will appear to you." **7** Moses said to Aaron, "**Draw near to the altar**, and offer your sin offering, and your burnt offering, and make atonement for yourself, and for the people; and offer the offering of the people, and **make atonement for them**, as Yahweh commanded."

8 So Aaron came near to the altar, and killed the calf of the sin offering, which was for himself. **9** The sons of Aaron presented the blood to him; and he dipped his finger in the blood, and put it on the horns of the altar, and **poured out the blood at the base of the altar**; **10** but the fat, and the kidneys, and the cover from the liver of the sin offering, he burned upon the altar, as Yahweh commanded Moses. **11** The flesh and the skin he burned with fire outside the camp.

12 He killed the burnt offering; and Aaron's sons delivered the blood to him, and he sprinkled it around on the altar. **13** **They delivered the burnt offering** to him, piece by piece, and the **head**. He burned them upon the altar. **14** He washed the innards and the legs and burned them on the burnt offering on the altar.

Rom 3:21 But now apart from the law, a **righteousness of God has been revealed**, being testified by the law and the prophets; **22** even the righteousness of God through faith in Jesus Christ to all and on all those who believe. For there is no distinction, **23** for all have sinned, and fall short of the glory of God; **24** being justified freely by his grace through the redemption that is in Christ Jesus, **25** whom God sent to be **an atoning sacrifice** through **faith in his blood**, for a demonstration of his righteousness through the passing over of prior sins, in God's forbearance; **26** to **demonstrate his righteousness** at this present time, that he might himself be just and the justifier of him who has faith in **Jesus**.

NOTE: While not called out as a specific echo, the word "glory" in Romans 3:23 clearly echoes the word "glory" in Leviticus 9:6. The last echo is proposed because Jesus is the head (Colossians 1:18).

Lev 9:15 He presented the people's offering, and took the goat of the <u>sin</u> offering, which was for the people, and killed it, and offered it for sin, like the first. **16** He presented the burnt offering and offered it according to the ordinance. **17** He presented the meal offering, filled his hand from there, and burned it upon the altar, in addition to the burnt offering of the morning.

18 He also killed the bull and the ram, the sacrifice of peace offerings, which was for the people. Aaron's sons delivered to him the blood, which he sprinkled around on the altar; **19** and the fat of the bull and of the ram, the fat tail, and that which covers the innards, and the kidneys, and the cover of the liver; **20** and they put the fat upon the breasts, and he burned the fat on the altar. **21** Aaron waved the breasts and the right thigh for a **wave offering before Yahweh**, as Moses commanded.

Rom 3:27 Where then is the **<u>boasting</u>**? It is excluded. By what kind of law? Of works? No, but **by a law of faith**.

NOTE: The word "sin" is proposed to echo the word "boasting" since the root of all sin is considered to be pride.

Lev 9:22 Aaron lifted up his hands toward the people and blessed them; and he came down from offering the sin offering, and the burnt offering, and the peace offerings. **23** Moses and Aaron went into the Tent of Meeting, and came out, and **blessed the people**; and Yahweh's glory **<u>appeared to all the people</u>**. **24** Fire came out from before Yahweh and consumed the burnt offering and the fat on the altar. **When all the people saw it**, they **<u>shouted and fell on their faces</u>**.

Rom 3:28 We maintain therefore that a man is justified by faith apart from the works of the law. **29** Or is God **the God of Jews only**? Isn't he the God of Gentiles also? **<u>Yes, of Gentiles also</u>**, **30** since indeed there is one God who will justify the **circumcised by faith and the uncircumcised through faith**. **31** Do we then nullify the law through faith? May it never be! No, **<u>we establish the law</u>**.

Leviticus 10

Romans 4

Lev 10:1 Nadab and Abihu, the sons of Aaron, each took his censer, and put fire in it, and laid incense on it, and **offered strange fire before Yahweh**, which he had not commanded them. **2** Fire came out from before Yahweh, and devoured them, and they died before Yahweh. **3** Then Moses said to Aaron, "This is what Yahweh spoke of, saying, 'I will show myself holy to those who come near me, and before all the people I will be glorified.'" Aaron held his peace.

4 Moses called Mishael and Elzaphan, the sons of Uzziel the uncle of Aaron, and said to them, "Draw near, carry your brothers from before the sanctuary out of the camp." **5** So they came near, and carried them in their tunics out of the camp, as Moses had said. **6** Moses said to Aaron, and to Eleazar and to Ithamar, his sons, "Don't let the hair of your heads go loose, and don't tear your clothes, so that you don't die, and so that he is not angry with all the congregation; but let your brothers, the whole house of Israel, bewail the burning which Yahweh has kindled. **7** <u>You shall not go out from the door</u> of the Tent of Meeting, lest you die; for the **anointing oil of Yahweh is on you**." They did according to the word of Moses.

Rom 4:1 What then will we say that Abraham, our forefather, has found according to the flesh? **2 For if Abraham was justified by works, he has something to boast about, but not toward God**. **3** For what does the Scripture say? "Abraham believed God, and it was accounted to him for righteousness." **4** Now to him who works, the reward is not counted as grace, but as something owed. **5** But to him **who doesn't work**, but **believes in him** who justifies the ungodly, his faith is accounted for righteousness.

NOTE: It can be said that Romans 4:5 is the summary of all the verses in Leviticus 10:1-7. Nadab and Abihu took matters into their own hands (i.e. their works) rather than resting with faith in God's perfect plan.

Lev 10:8 Yahweh spoke to Aaron, saying, **9** "You and your sons are not to drink wine or strong drink whenever you go into the Tent of Meeting, or you will die. This shall be a statute forever throughout your generations. **10** You are to make a **distinction** between the holy and the common, and between the unclean and the clean. **11** You are to teach the children of Israel all the statutes which Yahweh has spoken to them by Moses."

12 Moses spoke to Aaron, and to Eleazar and to Ithamar, his sons who were left, "Take the meal offering that remains of the offerings of Yahweh made by fire, and eat it without yeast beside the altar; for it is most holy; **13** and you shall eat it in a holy place, because it is your portion, and your sons' portion, of the offerings of Yahweh made by fire; for so I am commanded. **14** The waved breast and the heaved thigh you shall eat in a clean place, you, and your sons, and your daughters with you: for they are given as your portion, and your sons' portion, out of the sacrifices of the peace offerings of the children of Israel. **15** They shall bring the heaved thigh and the waved breast with the offerings made by fire of the fat, to wave it for a wave offering before Yahweh. It shall be yours, and your sons' with you, as a portion forever, as Yahweh has commanded."

16 Moses diligently inquired about the **goat of the sin offering**, and behold, it was burned. He was angry with Eleazar and with Ithamar, the sons of Aaron who were left, saying, **17** "Why haven't you eaten the sin offering in the place of the sanctuary, since it is most holy, and he has given it to you to bear the iniquity of the congregation, to make atonement for them before Yahweh? **18** Behold, its blood was not brought into the inner part of the sanctuary. You should certainly have eaten it in the sanctuary, as I commanded." **19** Aaron spoke to Moses, "**Behold, today they have offered their sin offering and their burnt offering before Yahweh; and such things as these have happened to me. If I had eaten the sin offering today, would it have been pleasing in Yahweh's sight?**" **20** When Moses heard that, it was pleasing in his sight.

Rom 4:6 Even as David also pronounces blessing on the man to whom God counts righteousness **apart** from works: **7** "Blessed are they whose iniquities are forgiven, **whose sins are covered**.

8 Blessed is the man whom the Lord will by no means charge with sin."

Leviticus 11	Romans 4:9
Lev 11:1 Yahweh spoke to Moses and to Aaron, saying to them, **2** "Speak to the children of Israel, saying, '<u>**These are the living things which you may eat**</u> among all the animals that are on the earth. **3** Whatever parts the hoof, and is cloven-footed, and chews the cud among the animals, that you may eat. **4** "'Nevertheless these you shall not eat of those that chew the cud, or of those who part the hoof: the camel, because it chews the cud but doesn't have a parted hoof, is <u>unclean to you</u>. **5** The hyrax, because it chews the cud but doesn't have a parted hoof, is <u>unclean to you</u>. **6** The hare, because it chews the cud but doesn't have a parted hoof, is <u>unclean to you</u>. **7** The pig, because it has a split hoof, and is cloven-footed, but doesn't chew the cud, is <u>unclean to you</u>. **8** You shall not eat their meat. You shall not touch their carcasses. They are <u>unclean to you</u>.	**Rom 4:9** <u>**Is this blessing then pronounced only on the circumcised, or also on the uncircumcised?**</u> For we say that faith was accounted to Abraham for righteousness. **10** How then was it counted? When he was in circumcision, or in <u>uncircumcision</u>? Not in circumcision, but in <u>uncircumcision</u>. **11** He received the sign of circumcision, a seal of the righteousness of the faith which he had while he was in <u>uncircumcision</u>, that he might be the father of all those who believe, though they might be in <u>uncircumcision</u>, that righteousness might also be accounted to them. **12** He is the father of circumcision to those who not only are of the circumcision, but who also walk in the steps of that faith of our father Abraham, which he had in <u>uncircumcision</u>.

NOTE: After their opening summary statements, both Leviticus and Romans use the words "unclean to you" and "uncircumcision" five times respectively in this pairing. The Jewish people did not receive the commands regarding kosher eating until after the Red Sea crossing. Said another way, they did not eat kosher until after they "believed God would save them." Similarly, Abraham's faith, which was credited to him as righteousness, came before receiving the covenant of circumcision, not after. A covenant is structured in five parts, and the Ten Commandments were written on two tablets with five commandments on each.

Lev 11:9 "'These you may eat of all that are in the waters: whatever has fins and scales in the waters, in the seas, and in the rivers, that you may eat. **10** All that don't have fins and scales in the seas and in the rivers, of all that move in the waters, and of all the living creatures that are in the waters, they are an abomination to you, **11** and you shall detest them. You shall not eat of their meat, and you shall detest their carcasses. **12** Whatever has no fins nor scales in the waters is an abomination to you.

13 "'<u>These you shall detest among the birds; they shall not be eaten because they are an abomination</u>: the eagle, the vulture, the black vulture, **14** the red kite, any kind of black kite, **15** any kind of raven, **16** the horned owl, the screech owl, the gull, any kind of hawk, **17** the little owl, the cormorant, the great owl, **18** the white owl, the desert owl, the osprey, **19** the stork, any kind of heron, the hoopoe, and the bat.

20 "'All flying insects that walk on all fours are an abomination to you. **21** Yet you may eat these: of all winged creeping things that go on all fours, which have jointed legs above their feet, with which to hop on the earth. **22** Even of these you may eat: any kind of locust, any kind of katydid, any kind of cricket, and any kind of grasshopper. **23** But all winged creeping things which have four feet are an abomination to you.

Rom 4:13 For the promise to Abraham and to his offspring that he would be heir of the world wasn't through the law, but through the righteousness of faith. **14** For if those who are of the law are heirs, faith is made void, and the promise is made of no effect. **15** <u>For the law produces wrath</u>; for where there is no law, neither is there disobedience.

Lev 11:24 "'By these you will become unclean: whoever touches their carcass shall be unclean until the evening. **25** Whoever carries any part of their carcass shall wash his clothes and be unclean until the evening. **26** "'Every animal which has a split hoof that isn't completely divided, or doesn't chew the cud, is unclean to you. Everyone who touches them shall be unclean. **27** Whatever goes on its paws, among all animals that go on all fours, they are unclean to you. Whoever touches their carcass shall be unclean until the evening. **28** He who carries their carcass shall wash his clothes and be unclean until the evening. They are unclean to you.

29 "'These are they which are unclean to you among the creeping things that creep on the earth: the weasel, the rat, any kind of great lizard, **30** the gecko, and the monitor lizard, the wall lizard, the skink, and the chameleon. **31** These are they which are unclean to you among all that creep. Whoever touches them when they are **dead** shall be unclean until the evening. **32** Anything they fall on when they are dead shall be unclean; whether it is any vessel of wood, clothing, or skin, or sack, whatever vessel it is, with which any work is done, it must be put into water, and it shall be unclean until the evening. Then it will be clean. **33** Every earthen vessel into which any of them falls, whatever is in it shall be unclean, and you shall break it. **34** All food which may be eaten which is soaked in water shall be unclean. All drink that may be drunk in every such vessel shall be unclean. **35** Everything whereupon part of their carcass falls shall be unclean; whether oven, or range for pots, it shall be broken in pieces. They are unclean and shall be unclean to you. **36** Nevertheless a spring or a cistern in which water is gathered shall be clean, but that which touches their carcass shall be unclean. **37** If part of their carcass falls on any sowing **seed** which is to be sown, it is clean. **38** But if water is put on the **seed**, and part of their carcass falls on it, it is unclean to you.

Rom 4:16 For this cause, it is of faith, that it may be according to grace, to the end that the promise may be sure to all the offspring, not to that only which is of the law, but to that also which is of the faith of Abraham, who is the father of us all. **17** As it is written, "I have made you a father of many nations." This is in the presence of him whom he believed: God, who gives life to the **dead**, and calls the things that are not, as though they were. **18** Against hope, Abraham in hope believed, to the end that he might become a **father of many nations**, according to that which had been spoken, "So will your **offspring** be."

Lev 11:39 "'If any animal of which you may eat **dies**, he who touches its carcass shall be unclean until the evening. **40** He who eats of its carcass shall wash his clothes and be unclean until the evening. He also who carries its carcass shall wash his clothes and be unclean until the evening.

41 "'Every creeping thing that creeps on the earth is an abomination. It shall not be eaten. **42** Whatever goes on its belly, and whatever goes on all fours, or whatever has many feet, even all creeping things that creep on the earth, them you shall not eat; for they are an abomination. **43** You shall not make yourselves abominable with any creeping thing that creeps. You shall not make yourselves unclean with them, that you should be defiled by them.

Rom 4:19 He didn't become weak in faith. He didn't consider his own body, already having been worn out, (he being about a hundred years old), and the **deadness of Sarah's womb**. **20** Yet, looking to the promise of God, he didn't waver through unbelief, but grew strong through faith, giving glory to God, **21** and being fully assured that what he had promised, he was also able to perform. **22** Therefore it also was "credited to him for righteousness." **23** Now it was not written that it was accounted to him for his sake alone, **24** but for our sake also, to whom it will be accounted, who believe in him who raised Jesus our Lord from the dead, **25** who was delivered up for our trespasses, and was raised for our justification.

Leviticus 11:44	Romans 5
Lev 11:44 For I am **Yahweh your God**. Sanctify yourselves **therefore and be holy**; for **I am holy**. You shall not defile yourselves with any kind of creeping thing that moves on the earth.	Rom 5:1 Being therefore justified by faith, we have peace with **God through our Lord Jesus** Christ; 2 through whom we also have our **access by faith into this grace in which we stand**. We rejoice in hope of the **glory of God**.
Lev 11:45 For I am Yahweh who brought you up **out of the land of Egypt**, to be your God. You shall therefore be holy, for **I am holy**.	Rom 5:3 Not only that, but we also rejoice in our sufferings, knowing that **suffering produces perseverance**; 4 and perseverance, proven character; and proven character, hope; 5 and hope doesn't disappoint us, because God's love has been poured into our hearts through the **Holy Spirit** who was given to us.
Lev 11:46 "'This is the law of the animal, and of the bird, and of every living creature that moves in the waters, and of every creature that creeps on the earth, **47 to make a distinction between the unclean and the clean**, and between the living thing that may be eaten and the living thing that may not be eaten.'"	Rom 5:6 For while we were yet weak, at the right time **Christ died for the ungodly. 7 For one will hardly die for a righteous man**. Yet perhaps for a good person someone would even dare to die. 8 But God commends his own love toward us, in that while we were yet sinners, Christ died for us.

NOTE: [Shemini ends.] Paul makes a distinction between how hard it is to die for a righteous man, much less the ungodly. This parallels the distinction being made by God between clean and unclean animals.

Leviticus 12

Romans 5:9

Lev 12:1 Yahweh spoke to Moses, saying, **2** "Speak to the children of Israel, saying, 'If a woman conceives, and bears a male child, then she shall be unclean seven days; as in the days of her monthly period she shall be unclean. **3** In the eighth day the flesh of his foreskin shall be circumcised. **4** She shall continue in the **blood of purification** thirty-three days. She shall not touch any holy thing, nor come into the sanctuary, until the days of her purification are completed. **5** But if she bears a female child, then she shall be unclean two weeks, as in her period; and she shall continue in the blood of purification sixty-six days.

6 "'When the days of her purification are completed for a son or for a daughter, **she shall bring to the priest at the door of the Tent of Meeting, a year-old lamb** for a burnt offering, and a young pigeon or a turtledove, for a sin offering. **7** He shall offer it before Yahweh and make atonement for her; then she shall be cleansed from the fountain of her blood. "'This is the law for her who bears, whether a **male or a female**. **8** If she cannot afford a lamb, then she shall take two turtledoves or two young pigeons: the one for a burnt offering, and the other for a sin offering. **The priest shall make atonement for her**, and she shall be clean.'"

Rom 5:9 Much more then, being now **justified by his blood**, we will be saved from God's wrath through him. **10** For if while we were enemies, we were reconciled to God through the death of his Son, **much more, being reconciled, we will be saved by his life**. **11** Not only so, but we also rejoice in God through our Lord Jesus Christ, through whom we have now received the reconciliation.

12 Therefore as sin entered into the world through one man, and death through sin; so death passed to **all men**, because all sinned. **13** For until the law, sin was in the world; but sin is not charged when there is no law. **14** Nevertheless death reigned from Adam until Moses, even over those whose sins weren't like Adam's disobedience, who is a **foreshadowing of him who was to come**.

NOTE: [Tazria.] The "year old lamb" is to be brought *alive* to the priest, paralleling how we being reconciled by his death will be saved by his *life* – Christ the lamb of God.

Leviticus 13   Rom. 5:15

Lev 13:1 Yahweh spoke to Moses and to Aaron, saying, **2** "When a man shall have a swelling in his body's skin, or a scab, or a bright spot, and it becomes in the skin of his body the **plague of leprosy**, then he shall be brought to Aaron the priest or to one of his sons, the priests. **3** The priest shall examine the plague in the skin of the body. If the hair in the plague has turned white, and the appearance of the plague is deeper than the body's skin, it is the **plague of leprosy**; so, the priest shall examine him and pronounce him unclean. **4** If the bright spot is white in the skin of his body, and its appearance isn't deeper than the skin, and its hair hasn't turned white, then the priest shall isolate the person who has the plague for seven days. **5** The priest shall examine him on the **seventh day**. Behold, if in his eyes the plague is arrested and the plague hasn't spread in the skin, then the priest shall isolate him for seven more days. **6** The priest shall examine him again on the **seventh day**. Behold, if the plague has faded and the plague hasn't spread in the skin, then the priest shall pronounce him clean. It is a scab. He shall wash his clothes and be clean.

7 But if the scab spreads abroad in the skin after he has shown himself to the priest for his cleansing, he shall show himself to the priest again. **8** The priest shall examine him; and behold, if the scab has spread in the skin, then the priest shall pronounce him unclean. It is leprosy.

Rom 5:15 But the free gift isn't like the **trespass**. For if by the **trespass** of the one the many died, much more did the **grace** of God and the gift by the **grace** of the one man, Jesus Christ, abound to the many.

NOTE: The echo of leprosy by the concept of the trespass is consistently used here. Ever since Miriam contracted leprosy after speaking against Moses, (Numbers Ch. 12) Jewish people consider skin disease to be a sin of evil speech. Jesus said whatever proceeds out of the mouth defiles a man. (Matthew 15:11). The "seventh day" institute in Genesis as a sanctified day of rest seems to be echoed in the word "grace."

Lev 13:9 "When the plague of **leprosy is in a man**, then he shall be brought to the priest; **10** and the priest shall examine him. Behold, if there is a white swelling in the skin, and it has turned the hair white, and there is raw flesh in the swelling, **11** it is a **chronic leprosy** in the skin of his body, and the priest shall pronounce him unclean. He shall not isolate him, for he is unclean. **12** If the leprosy breaks out all over the skin, and the leprosy covers all the skin of the one who has the plague from his head even to his feet, as far as it appears to the priest, **13** then the priest shall examine him. Behold, if the leprosy has covered all his flesh, he shall pronounce him clean of the plague. **It has all turned white: he is clean**. **14** But whenever raw flesh appears in him, he shall be unclean. **15** The priest shall examine the raw flesh and pronounce him unclean: the raw flesh is unclean. It is *leprosy*. **16** Or if the raw flesh turns again, and **is changed to white**, then he shall come to the priest. **17** The priest shall examine him. **Behold, if the plague has turned white**, then the priest shall pronounce him clean of the plague. **He is clean**.

Rom 5:16 The gift is not as through **one who sinned**; for the judgment came by one to **condemnation**, but the **free gift followed many trespasses** to justification. **17** For if by the *trespass* of the one, death reigned through the one; so much more will those who receive the **abundance of grace** and of the **gift of righteousness** reign in life through the one, **Jesus Christ**.

NOTE: In the Leviticus passage, after having leprosy, suddenly the person's flesh turns white, and he is declared clean. Similarly, after sin and condemnation, we can receive the abundance of grace and the gift of righteousness (i.e. cleansing).

Lev 13:18 "When the body has **a boil on its skin**, and it has healed, **19** and in the place of the boil there is a white swelling, or a bright spot, white, and somewhat reddish, then it shall be shown to the priest; **20** and the priest shall examine it. Behold, if its appearance is lower than the skin, and its hair has turned white, then the priest shall pronounce him unclean. It is the plague of leprosy. It has broken out in the boil. **21** But if the priest examines it, and behold, there are no white hairs in it, and it isn't deeper than the skin, but is dim, then the priest shall isolate him seven days. **22** If it spreads in the skin, then the priest shall pronounce him unclean. **It is a plague**. **23** But if the bright spot stays in its place, and hasn't spread, it is the scar from the boil; and the priest shall pronounce him clean.

24 "Or when the body has a burn from fire on its skin, and the raw flesh of the burn becomes a bright spot, reddish-white, or white, **25** then the priest shall examine it; and behold, if the hair in the bright spot has turned white, and its appearance is deeper than the skin, it is leprosy. It has broken out in the burn, and the priest shall pronounce him unclean. It is the plague of leprosy. **26** But if the priest examines it, and behold, there is no white hair in the bright spot, and it isn't deeper than the skin, but has faded, then the priest shall isolate him seven days. **27** The priest shall examine him on the seventh day. If it has spread in the skin, then the priest shall pronounce him unclean. It is the plague of leprosy. **28** If the **bright spot stays in its place**, and has not spread in the skin, but is faded, it is the swelling from the burn, and the priest shall **pronounce him clean**, for it is the scar from the burn.

Rom 5:18 So then as through **one trespass**, all men were **condemned**; even so through **one act of righteousness**, all men were **justified** to life.

NOTE: A single outbreak on one person can potentially spread creating a plague. This echoes the idea of "through one trespass, all men were condemned."

Lev 13:29 "When a <u>man</u> or a woman has a plague on the head or on the beard, **30** then the priest shall examine the plague; and behold, if its appearance is deeper than the skin, and the hair in it is yellow and thin, then the priest shall pronounce him unclean. It is an itch. It is leprosy of the head or of the beard. **31** If the priest examines the plague of itching, and behold, its appearance isn't deeper than the skin, and there is no black hair in it, then the priest shall isolate the person infected with itching seven days. **32** On the seventh day the priest shall examine the plague; and behold, if the itch hasn't spread, and there is no yellow hair in it, and the appearance of the itch isn't deeper than the skin, **33** then he shall be shaved, but he shall not shave the itch. Then the priest shall isolate the one who has the itch seven more days. **34** On the seventh day, the priest shall examine the itch; and behold, if the itch hasn't spread in the skin, and its appearance isn't deeper than the skin, then the priest shall pronounce him clean. He shall wash his clothes and be clean. **35** But if the itch spreads in the skin after his cleansing, **36** then the priest shall examine him; and behold, if the itch has spread in the skin, the priest shall not look for the yellow hair; he is unclean. **37** But if in his eyes the itch is arrested and black hair has grown in it, the itch is healed. He is clean. The priest shall pronounce him clean.

38 "When a man or a woman has bright spots in the skin of the body, even white bright spots, **39** then the priest shall examine them. Behold, if the bright spots on the skin of their body are a dull white, it is a harmless rash. It has broken out in the skin. He is clean.

40 "If a man's hair has fallen from his head, he is bald. He is clean. **41** If his hair has fallen off from the front part of his head, he is forehead bald. He is clean. **42** But if there is in the bald head or the bald forehead a reddish-white plague, it is leprosy breaking out in his bald head or his bald forehead. **43** Then the priest shall examine him. Behold, if the swelling of the plague is reddish-white in his bald head, or in his bald forehead, like the appearance of leprosy in the skin of the body, **44** he is a leprous <u>man</u>. He is unclean. The priest shall surely pronounce him unclean. His plague is on his head.

45 "<u>**The leper in whom the plague is shall wear torn clothes, and the hair of his head shall hang loose. He shall cover his upper lip, and shall cry, 'Unclean! Unclean!**</u>'" **46** All the days in which the plague is in him he shall be unclean. He is unclean. He shall dwell alone. Outside of **the camp** shall be his dwelling.

Rom 5:19 For as through the <u>one man's</u> disobedience **many were made sinners**, even so through the obedience of the one, **many** will be made righteous.

NOTE: Paul writes about how one man's disobedience cause many to be made sinners. In Leviticus, one man's disobedience to isolate when having leprosy, can cause an outbreak on all. The accounts echo each other.

Lev 13:47 "The garment also that the **plague of leprosy** is in, whether it is a woolen garment, or a linen garment; **48** whether it is in warp or woof; of linen or of wool; whether in a leather, or in anything made of leather; **49** if the plague is greenish or reddish in the garment, or in the leather, or in the warp, or in the woof, or in anything made of leather; it is the plague of leprosy, and shall be shown to the priest. **50** The priest shall examine the plague and isolate the plague seven days. **51** He shall examine the plague on the seventh day. If the plague has spread in the garment, either in the warp, or in the woof, or in the leather, whatever use the leather is used for, the plague is a destructive mildew. It is unclean. **52** He shall burn the garment, whether the warp or the woof, in wool or in linen, or anything of leather, in which the plague is, for it is a destructive mildew. It shall be burned in the fire.

53 "If the priest examines it, and behold, the plague hasn't spread in the garment, either in the warp, or in the woof, or in anything of leather; **54** then the priest shall command that they wash the thing in which the plague is, and he shall isolate it seven more days. **55** Then the priest shall examine it, after the plague is washed; and behold, if the plague hasn't changed its color, and the plague hasn't spread, it is unclean; you shall burn it in the fire. It is a mildewed spot, whether the bareness is inside or outside.

56 If the priest looks, and behold, the plague has faded after it is washed, then he shall tear it out of the garment, or out of the leather, or out of the warp, or out of the woof; **57** and if it appears again in the garment, either in the warp, or in the woof, or in anything of leather, it is spreading. You shall burn the garment in which the plague is with fire. **58** The garment, either the warp, or the woof, or whatever thing of leather it is, which you shall wash, if the plague has departed from them, **then it shall be washed the second time, and it will be clean**." **59** This is the **law of the plague** of mildew in a garment of wool or linen, either in the warp, or the woof, or in anything of leather, for pronouncing it **clean** or unclean.

Rom 5:20 The law came in that **the trespass might abound**; but where sin abounded, **grace abounded more exceedingly**; **21** that as **sin reigned in death**, even so grace might reign through **righteousness** to eternal life through Jesus Christ our Lord.

NOTE: [Tazria ends.]

Leviticus 14   Romans 6

Lev 14:1 Yahweh spoke to Moses, saying, **2** "This shall be the law of the leper in the day of his cleansing: He shall be brought to the priest, **3** and the priest shall go out of the camp. The priest **shall examine him**. Behold, if the plague of leprosy is healed in the leper, **4** then the priest shall command them to take for him who is to be cleansed two living clean birds, cedar wood, scarlet, and hyssop. **5** The priest shall command them to <u>kill one of the birds</u> in an earthen vessel over running water. **6** As for the living bird, he shall take it, the cedar wood, the scarlet, and the hyssop, and shall dip them and the living bird in the blood of the bird that was killed over the running water. **7** He shall sprinkle on him who is to be cleansed from the leprosy seven times, and shall pronounce him clean, and shall let the **living** bird go into the open field. **8** "He who is to be cleansed shall wash his clothes, and shave off all his hair, and **bathe himself in water**; and he shall be clean. After that he shall come into the camp but shall dwell outside his tent seven days. **9** It shall be on the seventh day that he shall shave all his hair off his head and his beard and his eyebrows. He shall shave all his hair. He shall wash his clothes, and he shall **bathe his body in water**. Then he shall be clean.

10 "On the eighth day he shall take two male lambs without defect, one ewe lamb a year old without defect, three tenths of an ephah of fine flour for a meal offering, mixed with oil, and one log of oil. **11** The priest who cleanses him shall set the man who is to be cleansed, and those things, before Yahweh, at the door of the Tent of Meeting. **12** The priest shall take one of the male lambs, and offer him for a trespass offering, with the log of oil, and wave them for a wave offering before Yahweh. **13** He shall **kill the male lamb** in the place where they kill the sin offering and the burnt offering, in the place of the sanctuary; for as the sin offering is the priest's, so is the trespass offering. It is most holy.

Rom 6:1 What shall we say then? **Shall we continue in sin**, that grace may abound? **2** May it never be! We who <u>died</u> to sin, how could we **live** in it any longer? **3** Or don't you know that all we who were **baptized** into Christ Jesus were **baptized** into his **death**?

NOTE: [Metzora.] Prior to this point in Leviticus the word bathe (*rachats* in Hebrew), has only been used once for washing people (Lev. 8:6). But starting in Lev. 14, bathing in water is a major theme. Consequently, in Romans 6:3 Paul begins to discuss baptism, and twice uses the word baptized (*baptizo* in Greek), the only two mentions in Romans.

Lev 14:14 The priest shall take some of the blood of the trespass offering, and the priest shall put it on the tip of the right ear of him who is to be cleansed, and on the thumb of his right hand, and on the big toe of his right foot. **15** The priest shall take some of the log of oil and pour it into the palm of his own left hand. **16** The priest shall dip his right finger in the oil that is in his left hand and shall sprinkle some of the oil with his finger seven times before Yahweh. **17** The priest shall put some of the rest of the oil that is in his hand on the tip of the right ear of him who is to be cleansed, and on the thumb of his right hand, and on the big toe of his right foot, upon the blood of the trespass offering. **18** The rest of the oil that is in the priest's hand he shall put on the head of him who is to be cleansed, and the priest shall make atonement for him before Yahweh. **19** The priest shall offer the sin offering and make atonement for him who is to be cleansed because of his uncleanness. Afterward he shall **kill the burnt offering**; **20** then the priest shall offer the burnt offering and the meal offering on the altar. The priest shall make atonement for him, and he shall be clean.

21 "If he is poor, and can't afford so much, then he shall take one male lamb for a trespass **offering to be waved**, to make atonement for him, and one tenth of an ephah of fine flour mixed with oil for a meal offering, and a log of oil; **22** and two turtledoves, or two young pigeons, such as he is able to afford; and the one shall be a sin offering, and the other a burnt offering. **23** On the eighth day he shall bring them for his cleansing to the priest, to the door of the **Tent of Meeting, before Yahweh**. **24** The priest shall take the lamb of the trespass offering, and the log of oil, and the priest shall wave them for a wave offering before Yahweh. **25** He shall kill the lamb of the trespass offering. The priest shall take some of the blood of the trespass offering and put it on the tip of the right ear of him who is to be cleansed, and on the thumb of his right hand, and on the big toe of his right foot. **26** The priest shall pour some of the oil into the palm of his own left hand; **27** and the priest shall sprinkle with his right finger some of the oil that is in his left hand seven times before Yahweh. **28** The priest shall put some of the oil that is in his hand on the tip of the right ear of him who is to be cleansed, and on the thumb of his right hand, and **on the big toe of his right foot, on the place of the blood of the trespass offering**. **29** The rest of the oil that is in the priest's hand he shall put on the head of him who is to be cleansed, to make atonement for him before Yahweh.

Rom 6:4 We were buried therefore with him through baptism into **death**, that just as Christ was **raised** from the dead through the **glory of the Father**, so we also might **walk in newness of life**.

NOTE: Continuing on from the previous note, Paul uses the noun baptism (*baptisma* in Greek) only once in Romans 6:4. The echo of "baptism" is suggested to be "cleansed" which receives support from Acts 22:16 and 1 Peter 3:21. Regarding the phrase in Leviticus "offering to be waved" which is proposed to echo the word "raised," it is observed that for an object must be raised before it is waved.

Lev 14:30 He shall offer one of the turtledoves, or of the young pigeons, such as he is able to afford, **31** even such as he is able to afford, the one for a sin offering, and the other for a burnt offering, with the meal offering. The priest shall make atonement for him who is to be cleansed before Yahweh. **32** This is the law for him in whom is the plague of leprosy, who is not able to afford the sacrifice for his cleansing.

33 Yahweh spoke to Moses and to Aaron, saying, **34** "When **you have come** into the land of Canaan, which I give to you for a possession, and I put a spreading mildew in a **house** in the land of your possession, **35** then he who owns the house shall come and tell the priest, saying, 'There seems to me to be some sort of plague in the house.' **36** The priest shall command that they empty the house, before the **priest goes in to examine the plague,** that all that is in the house not be made unclean. Afterward the priest shall go in to inspect the house.

Rom 6:5 For if **we have become united** with him in the **likeness of his death**, we will also be part of his resurrection;

NOTE: When we are buried with Christ we are united with him in the likeness of his death. In the same way the priest goes into the house that has a plague caused by sin.

Lev 14:37 He shall examine the plague; and behold, if the plague is in the walls of the house with hollow streaks, greenish or reddish, and it appears to be deeper than the wall, **38** then the priest shall go out of the house to the door of the house and shut up the house seven days. **39** The priest shall come again on the seventh day, and look. If the plague has spread in the walls of the house, **40** then the priest shall command that they take out the stones in which is the plague and cast them into an unclean place outside of the city. **41** He shall cause the inside of the house to be scraped all over. They shall **pour out the mortar that they scraped** off outside of the city into an unclean place. **42** They shall take other stones and put them in the place of those stones; and he shall take other mortar and shall **plaster the house**.

43 "If the plague comes again and breaks out in the house after he has taken out the stones, and after he has scraped the house, and after it was plastered, **44** then the priest shall come in and look; and behold, if the plague has spread in the house, it is a destructive mildew in the house. It is unclean. **45** He shall <u>break down the house</u>, its stones, and its timber, and all the house's mortar. He shall **carry them out of the city** into an unclean place. **46** Moreover he who goes into the house while it is shut up shall be unclean until the evening. **47** <u>**He who lies in the house**</u> shall wash his clothes; and he who eats in the house shall wash his clothes. **48** "If the priest shall come in, and examine it, and behold, the plague hasn't spread in the house, after the house was plastered, then the priest shall pronounce **the house clean**, because the <u>**plague is healed**</u>.

Rom 6:6 knowing this, that our old man was crucified with him, that the **body of sin might be done away with**, so that we would <u>**no longer be in bondage**</u> to sin. **7** For he who has <u>died</u> has been **freed from sin**.

8 But if <u>**we died with Christ**</u>, we believe that **we will also live with him**, **9** knowing that Christ, being raised from the dead, dies no more. <u>**Death no longer has dominion**</u> over him!

NOTE: In Romans 6:8, "we died with Christ" is echoed in Leviticus 14:47 by "he who lies in the house". The word lies can also be translated as "sleeps".

Lev 14:49 To cleanse the house he shall take two birds, cedar wood, scarlet, and hyssop. **50** He shall **kill one of the birds** in an earthen vessel over running water. **51** He shall take the cedar wood, the hyssop, the scarlet, and the living bird, and dip them in the blood of the slain bird, and in the running water, and sprinkle the house seven times. **52** He shall cleanse the house with the blood of the bird, and with the running water, with the living bird, with the cedar wood, with the hyssop, and with the scarlet; **53** but he shall let the **living bird go out** of the city into the open field. So shall he make **atonement for the house; and it shall be clean.**"

54 This is the law for any plague of leprosy, and for an itch, **55** and for the leprosy of a garment, and for a house; **56** and for a swelling, and for a scab, and for a bright spot; **57** to teach when it is unclean, and when it is clean. This is the law of leprosy.

Rom 6:10 For the **death that he died**, he died to sin one time; but the **life that he lives**, he lives to God. **11** Thus consider yourselves also to be **dead to sin, but alive to God** in Christ Jesus our Lord.

NOTE: A profound echo is present. In Romans 6:10 Paul sees death and life in Christ in the two birds, and later in Rom. 7:4, two goats.

Leviticus 15   Romans 6:12

Lev 15:1 Yahweh spoke to Moses and to Aaron, saying, **2** "Speak to the children of Israel, and tell them, 'When any man has a discharge from his body, **because of his discharge he is unclean**. **3** This shall be his uncleanness in his discharge: whether his body runs with his discharge, or his body is stopped from his discharge, it is his uncleanness. **4** "'<u>Every bed</u> on which he who has the discharge lies shall be unclean; and everything he sits on shall be unclean. **5** Whoever **touches** his bed shall wash his clothes, and bathe himself in water, and be unclean until the evening. **6** He who sits on anything on which the man who has the discharge sat shall wash his clothes, and bathe himself in water, and be unclean until the evening. **7** "'He who touches the body of him who has the discharge shall wash his clothes, and bathe himself in water, and be unclean until the evening. **8** "'If he who has the discharge spits on him who is clean, then he shall wash his clothes, and bathe himself in water, and be unclean until the evening. **9** "'Whatever <u>saddle</u> he who has the discharge rides on shall be unclean. **10** Whoever **touches** anything that was under him shall be unclean until the evening. He who carries those things shall wash his clothes, and bathe himself in water, and be unclean until the evening. **11** "'Whomever he who has the discharge touches, without having rinsed his hands in water, he shall wash his clothes, and bathe himself in water, and be unclean until the evening. **12** "'The <u>earthen vessel</u>, which he who has the discharge touches, shall be broken; and every **vessel of wood** shall be rinsed in water.

Rom 6:12 Therefore don't let **sin reign in your mortal body**, that you should **obey it in its lusts**. **13** Also, do not present your **members** to sin as instruments of unrighteousness, but **present yourselves** to God as alive from the dead, and your **members** as instruments of righteousness to God. **14** For sin will not have dominion over you, for you are not **under law**, but **under grace**.

NOTE: Some commentaries suggest that the sin of Leviticus 15 is Gonorrhea, i.e. sexual sin. Paul seems to agree. In Romans 6:13, "members" meaning hands or feet, echoes "touches" in Leviticus 15:4. In Lev. 15:12, a vessel of "wood" echoes "grace" because of the Ark (made of wood), which represents Christ.

Lev 15:13 "'When he who has a discharge is cleansed of his discharge, then he shall count to himself seven days for his cleansing and wash his clothes; and he shall bathe his flesh in running water and shall be clean. **14** On the **eighth day** he shall take two turtledoves, or two young pigeons, and **come before Yahweh** to the door of the Tent of Meeting and give them to the priest. **15** The priest shall offer them, the one for a sin offering, and the other for a burnt offering. The priest shall make atonement for him before Yahweh for his discharge.

16 "'If any man has an emission of semen, then he shall bathe all his flesh in water, and be unclean until the evening. **17** Every **garment and every skin** which the semen is on shall be washed with water and be unclean until the evening. **18** If a man lies with a woman and there is an emission of semen, they shall both bathe themselves in water and be unclean until the evening.

Rom 6:15 What then? Shall we sin because we are **not under law**, but __under grace__? May it never be! **16** Don't you know that when you **present yourselves as servants** and obey someone, you are the servants of whomever you obey, whether of sin to death, or of obedience to righteousness?

NOTE: The eighth day is the beginning of a new week since the cleansing, representing Christ who broke the curse of the law.

Lev 15:19 "'If a woman has a discharge, and her discharge in her flesh is blood, she shall be in her impurity seven days. Whoever touches her shall be unclean until the evening. **20** Everything that she lies on in her impurity shall be **unclean**. Everything also that she sits on shall be unclean. **21** Whoever touches her bed shall wash his clothes, and bathe himself in water, and be unclean until the evening. **22** Whoever touches anything that she sits on shall wash his clothes, and bathe himself in water, and be unclean until the evening. **23** If it is on the bed, or on anything she sits on, when he touches it, he shall be unclean until the evening. **24** "'If any man lies with her, and her monthly flow is on him, he shall be unclean seven days; and every bed he lies on shall be unclean.

25 "'If a woman has a discharge of her blood many days not in the time of her period, or if she has a discharge beyond the time of her period, all the days of the discharge of her uncleanness shall be as in the days of her period. She is unclean. **26** Every bed she lies on all the days of her discharge shall be to her as the bed of her period. Everything she sits on shall be unclean, as the uncleanness of her period. **27** Whoever touches these things shall be unclean and shall wash his clothes and bathe himself in water and be unclean until the evening. **28** "'But if she is cleansed of her discharge, then she shall count to herself seven days, and after that she shall be **clean**. **29** On the eighth day she shall take two turtledoves, or two young pigeons, and bring them to the priest, to the door of the Tent of Meeting. **30** The priest shall offer the one for a sin offering, and the other for a burnt offering; and the priest shall make atonement for her before Yahweh for the uncleanness of her discharge.

Rom 6:17 But thanks be to God that, whereas you were bondservants of **sin**, you became obedient from the heart to that form of teaching to which you were delivered. **18** Being made free from sin, you became bondservants of **righteousness**.

Lev 15:31 "'Thus you shall separate the **children of Israel** from their **uncleanness**, so they will not die in their **uncleanness when they defile** my tabernacle that is among them.'" **32** This is the law of him who has a **discharge**, and of him who has an emission of semen, so that he is **unclean** by it; **33** and of her who has her period, and of a **man or woman** who has a discharge, and of him who lies with her who is unclean.	**Rom 6:19** I speak in **human** terms because of the weakness of your flesh; for as you presented your members as servants to **uncleanness** and to **wickedness upon wickedness**, even so now present your members as servants to righteousness for sanctification. **20** For when you were servants of **sin**, you were free from righteousness. **21** What fruit then did you have at that time in the things of which you are now **ashamed**? For the end of those things is death. **22** But now, being made free from sin and having become **servants of God**, you have your fruit of sanctification and the result of eternal life.

NOTE: [Metzora ends.] In Leviticus 15:31, the children of Israel here are spoken of here in their natural form. Paul echoes that with "human" and clarifies that it is because of the weakness of the flesh. The proposed echo of "discharge" and "sin" is not to imply that menstruation or emission is inherently sin, but by Jewish law both of them make one unclean.

Leviticus 16

Romans 6:23

Lev 16:1 Yahweh spoke to Moses **after the death of the two sons of Aaron, when they came near before Yahweh, and died**; **2** and Yahweh said to Moses, "Tell Aaron your brother **not to come at just any time** into the Most Holy Place within the veil, before the mercy seat which is on the ark; **lest he die**; for I will appear in the cloud on the mercy seat. **3** "Aaron shall come into the sanctuary with a young bull for a sin offering, and a ram for a burnt offering. **4** He shall put on the holy linen tunic. He shall have the linen trousers on his body, and shall be girded with the linen sash, and he shall be clothed with the linen turban. These are the holy garments. He shall bathe his body in water and put them on. **5** He shall take from the congregation of the children of Israel two male goats for a sin offering, and one ram for a burnt offering. **6** "Aaron shall offer the bull of the sin offering, which is for himself, and make atonement for himself and for his house. **7** He shall take the two goats and set them before Yahweh at the door of the Tent of Meeting. **8** Aaron shall cast lots for the **two goats: one lot for Yahweh**, and **the other lot for the scapegoat**.

Rom 6:23 For the wages of sin is death, but the free gift of God is eternal life in Christ Jesus our Lord.

Romans 7

7:1 Or don't you know, brothers (for I speak to men who know the law), that the law has **dominion** over a man for as long as he lives? **2** For the woman that has a husband is bound by law to the husband while he lives, but if the **husband dies**, she is discharged from the law of the husband. **3** So then if, while the husband lives, she is joined to another man, she would be called an adulteress. But if the husband dies, she is free from the law, so that she is no adulteress, though she is joined to another man.

4 Therefore, my brothers, **you also were made dead to the law through the body of Christ**, that you would be joined to another, **to him who was raised from the dead**, that we might produce fruit to God.

NOTE: [Acharei Mot.] In Leviticus 16:1, Nadab and Abihu, two sons of Aaron, died when they offered strange fire to the Lord. The wages of their sin was literal death. In Lev. 16:2, Aaron was *not* able to come into the Most Holy place whenever he wanted but needed to abide by the law. In that sense the law had dominion over him. In Lev. 16:8, the two goats – one that was killed and one that was released into the wilderness – echo how we are first made dead to the law through the body of Christ and then joined to him who was raised and lives.

Lev 16:9 Aaron shall present the goat on which the lot fell for Yahweh and **offer him for a sin offering**. **10** But the goat on which the lot fell for the scapegoat shall be presented alive before Yahweh, to make atonement for him, **to send him away as the scapegoat into the wilderness**.

11 "Aaron shall present the bull of the sin offering, which is for himself, and shall make **atonement for himself** and for his house and shall kill the bull of the sin offering which is for himself. **12** He shall take a censer full of coals of **fire** from off the altar before Yahweh, and two handfuls of sweet incense beaten small, and bring it within the veil. **13** He shall put the incense on the **fire** before Yahweh, that the cloud of the incense may cover the mercy seat that is on the covenant, so that he will not die. **14** He shall take some of the blood of the bull and sprinkle it with his finger on the mercy seat on the east; **and before the mercy seat he shall sprinkle some of the blood with his finger seven times**. **15** "Then he shall kill the goat of the sin offering that is for the people, and bring his blood within the veil, and do with his blood as he did with the blood of the bull and sprinkle it on the mercy seat and before the mercy seat.

Rom 7:5 For when we were in the flesh, the sinful passions which were through the law worked in our members **to bring out fruit to death**. **6** But now we have been **discharged from the law**, having died to that in which we were held; so that we serve in **newness of the spirit**, and not in oldness of the letter.

7 What shall we say then? Is the law sin? May it never be! However, I wouldn't have known sin except through the law. For I wouldn't have known **coveting** unless the law had said, "You shall not covet." **8** But sin, finding occasion through the commandment, produced in me all kinds of **coveting**. For apart from the law, sin is dead. **9** I was alive apart from the law once, but when the commandment came, sin revived and I died. **10 The commandment, which was for life, this I found to be for death**; **11** for sin, finding occasion through the commandment, deceived me, and through it killed me.

NOTE: The phrase "atonement for himself" in Leviticus 16:11 echoed by "newness of the spirit" in Romans 7:6 is the first of a series of similar echoes in coming pairings. See Leviticus 16:24, 30, 32-34, 17:11. The echo of "fire" in Lev. 16:12-13 by "coveting" in Romans 7:7-8 suggests that the sin of Nadab and Abihu at its core may have included the coveting power or control over how future offerings were performed, reminiscent of God's lack of regard for Cain's offering in Genesis 4:5.

NOTE: The idea that the commandment of the law "which was for life," which Paul "found to be for death," is an echo of the actions to be taken by the priest at "the mercy seat" in Lev. 16:14, can be understood first as a matter of life and death for the high priest himself. A rope was tied around the high priest's waste or ankle so that if he died in the Holy of Holies due to unworthiness, his body could be pulled out without anyone else having to enter that sacred place (Jewish Virtual Library). Second, when compared with the glory and holiness of that place, Paul found more and more cause to condemn himself by comparison to that holiness. Paul may have also seen in Lev. 16:14-15 the mention of the blood of bulls and goats, knowing that the blood of bulls and goats does not have the power to cleanse (Hebrews 9:12-14). Paul knew that something more than the blood of bulls and goats is needed because it is impossible for the blood of bulls and goats to take away sins (Heb. 10:4).

Lev 16:16 He shall make atonement for the **Holy** Place, because of the uncleanness of the children of Israel, and because of their transgressions, even all their sins; and so, he shall do for the Tent of Meeting that dwells with them in the middle of their uncleanness. **17** No one shall be in the Tent of Meeting when he enters to make atonement in the **Holy** Place, until he comes out, and has made atonement for himself and for his household, and for all the assembly of Israel. **18** He shall go out to the altar that is before Yahweh and make atonement for it, and shall take some of the bull's blood, and some of the goat's blood, and put it around on the horns of the altar. **19 He shall sprinkle some of the blood on it with his finger seven times, and cleanse it, and make it holy from the uncleanness of the children of Israel.**

Rom 7:12 Therefore the law indeed is **holy**, and the commandment **holy**, righteous, and good. **13** Did then that which is good become death to me? May it never be! But sin, that it might be shown to be sin, was producing death in me through that which is good; **that through the commandment sin might become exceedingly sinful.** **14** For we know that the law is spiritual, but I am fleshly, sold under sin.

NOTE: This pairing continues to develop the thoughts noted above.

16:20 "When he has finished atoning for the Holy Place, the Tent of Meeting, and the altar, he shall present the live goat. **21** Aaron shall lay both his hands on the head of the live goat and confess over him all the iniquities of the children of Israel, and all their transgressions, even all their **sins**; and he shall **put them on the head of the goat** and shall send him away into the wilderness by the hand of a man who is ready. **22** The goat shall carry all their iniquities on himself to a solitary land, and he shall release the goat in the wilderness.

7:15 For I don't understand what I am doing. For I don't practice what I desire to do; but what I hate that I do. **16** But if what I don't desire, that I do, I consent to the law that it is good. **17** So now it is no more I that do it, but **sin** which dwells in me. **18** For I know that in me, **that is, in my flesh, dwells no good thing.** For desire is present with me, but I don't find it doing that which is good. **19** For the good which I desire, I don't do; but the evil which I don't desire, that I practice.

NOTE: This pairing continues to develop the thoughts noted above.

Lev 16:23 "Aaron shall come into the Tent of Meeting and_shall take off the linen garments_ which he put on when he went into the Holy Place and shall **leave them there**. **24** Then he shall bathe his body in water in a holy place, _and put on his garments_, and come out and offer his burnt offering and the burnt **offering of the people** and make _atonement for himself_ and for the people. **25** The fat of the sin offering he shall burn on the altar. **26** "He who lets the goat go as the scapegoat shall wash his clothes, and bathe his body in water, and afterward he shall come into the camp. **27** The bull for the sin offering, and the goat for the sin offering, whose blood was brought in to make atonement in the Holy Place, shall be carried **outside** the camp; and they shall **burn their skins, their flesh, and their dung with fire**. **28** He who burns them shall wash his clothes, and bathe his body in water, and afterward he shall come into the camp.

Rom 7:20 But **if what I don't desire**, I do, it is no more I that do it, but **sin which dwells in me**.

21 I find _then the law that, to me_, while I desire to do **good**, evil is present. **22** For I **delight in God's law after the inward person**, **23** but I see a different law in my members, warring against the law of my mind, and bringing me into captivity under the law of sin which is in my members. **24** What a wretched man I am! Who will deliver me **out** of the **body of this death**? **25** I thank God through Jesus Christ, our Lord! So then with the mind, I myself serve God's law, but with the flesh, sin's law.

NOTE: The echoes in this pairing are proposed in tentative form. An understanding of the sequence of actions taken by the priest after releasing the live goat is the key to understanding Paul's inspiration by Leviticus 16:23-28.

Leviticus 16:29	Romans 8
Lev 16:29 "It shall be a statute to you forever: in the seventh month, on the tenth day of the month, you shall afflict your souls, and **shall do no kind of work**, whether native-born or a foreigner who lives as a foreigner among you; **30** for on this day **shall atonement be made for you**, to cleanse you. **You shall be clean from all your sins before Yahweh**. **31** It is a Sabbath of solemn rest to you, and you shall afflict your souls. **It is a statute forever**.	**Rom 8:1** There is therefore now no condemnation to those who are in Christ Jesus, who **don't walk** according to the flesh, **but according to the Spirit**. **2** For the **law of the Spirit of life** in Christ Jesus made me **free** from the law of sin and of death.

NOTE: Paul echoes the law of Spirit of life in Christ Jesus in the Day of Atonement. While we can afflict our souls to move into a proper attitude, there is no "work" that we can achieve here in our own flesh, to enable the freedom that is desired. In Romans 8:2, the word "free" indicates that in Christ we don't need to wait for a certain day of the year to receive our atonement for sins. In Leviticus 16:31, what is described as a "statute forever" is seen by Paul as being forever free from the law of sin and death.

Lev 16:32 The priest, who is anointed and who is consecrated to be priest in his father's place, shall **make the atonement**, and shall put on the linen garments, even the holy garments. **33** He shall make atonement for the Holy Sanctuary; and he shall make atonement for the Tent of Meeting and for the altar; and he shall make atonement for the priests and for all the people of the assembly. **34** "This shall be an everlasting statute for you, to make atonement for the **children of Israel once in the year because of all their sins**." It was done as Yahweh commanded Moses.	**Rom 8:3** For what **the law couldn't do**, in that it was weak through the flesh, God did, **sending his own Son** in the likeness of sinful flesh and for sin, he condemned sin in the flesh, **4** that the ordinance of the law might be fulfilled in us who walk not after the flesh, but after the Spirit. **5** For those who live according to the flesh set their minds on the things of the flesh, but those who live according to the Spirit, the things of the Spirit. **6** For the mind of the flesh is death, but the mind of the Spirit is life and peace; **7** because the mind of the flesh is hostile toward God, for it is not subject to God's law, neither indeed can it be. **8** **Those who are in the flesh can't please God**.

NOTE: The anointed priest in Leviticus 16:32 is one of a series of successive priests. Yeshua is part of a generational line (Mat. 1:1) as well has Joshua the priest (Zechariah 3:1-9). In the Leviticus side of the pairing, the words "make atonement" are used **five** times. In the Romans side of the pairing, there is **one** use of "sending his own son" and followed by **four** uses of the word "spirit".

Leviticus 17   Romans 8:9

Lev 17:1 Yahweh spoke to Moses, saying, **2** "Speak to Aaron, and to his sons, and to all the children of Israel, and say to them, 'This is the thing which Yahweh has commanded: **3** Whatever man there is of the Louse of Israel who kills a bull, or lamb, or goat in the camp, or who kills it outside the camp, **4** and hasn't **brought it to the door of the Tent of Meeting to offer it as an offering to Yahweh** before Yahweh's tabernacle: blood shall be imputed to that man. He has shed blood. That man shall be **cut off from among his people**. **5** This is to the end that the children of Israel may bring their sacrifices, which they sacrifice in the open field, that they may bring them to Yahweh, to the door of the Tent of Meeting, to the priest, and sacrifice them for sacrifices of peace offerings to Yahweh. **6** The priest shall sprinkle the blood on the altar of Yahweh at the door of the Tent of Meeting and **burn the fat for a pleasant aroma to Yahweh**. **7** They shall no more sacrifice their sacrifices to the goat idols, after which they play the prostitute. This shall be a statute forever to them **throughout their generations**.'

Rom 8:9 But you are not in the flesh but in the Spirit, if indeed the **Spirit of God dwells in you**. But if any man doesn't have the Spirit of Christ, **he is not his**. **10** If Christ is in you, the body is dead because of sin, but **the spirit is alive because of righteousness**. **11** But if the Spirit of him who raised up Jesus from the dead dwells in you, he who raised up Christ Jesus from the dead will also **give life to your mortal bodies** through his Spirit who dwells in you.

NOTE: The echoes in this pairing are proposed in tentative form.

Lev 17:8 "You shall say to them, 'Any man there is of the house of Israel, or of the **strangers who live as foreigners among them**, who offers a burnt offering or sacrifice, **9** and doesn't bring it to the door of the Tent of Meeting to sacrifice it to Yahweh, that man shall be cut off from his people. **10** "'Any man of the house of Israel, or of the **strangers who live as foreigners among them**, who eats any kind of blood, I will set my face against that soul who eats blood and will cut him off from among his people. **11** For the life of the flesh is in the blood. I have given it to you on the altar to make atonement for your souls; for it is the blood that makes atonement by reason of the life. **12** Therefore I have said to the children of Israel, "No person among you may eat blood, nor may any **stranger who lives as a foreigner among you** eat blood." **13** "'Whatever man there is of the children of Israel, or of the **strangers who live as foreigners among them**, who takes in hunting any animal or bird that may be eaten, he shall pour out its blood, and cover it with dust.

14 For as to the life of all flesh, its blood is with its life. Therefore, I said to the children of Israel, "You shall not eat the blood of any kind of flesh; for the life of all flesh is its blood. Whoever eats it shall be cut off." **15** "'Every person that eats what dies of itself, or that which is torn by animals, whether he is native-born or a foreigner, shall wash his clothes, and bathe himself in water, and be unclean until the evening. Then he shall be clean. **16** But if he doesn't wash them, or bathe his flesh, then he shall bear his iniquity.'"

Rom 8:12 So then, brothers, we are debtors, not to the flesh, to live after the flesh. **13** For if you live after the flesh, you must die; but if by the Spirit you put to death the deeds of the body, you will live. **14** For as many as are led by the Spirit of God, these are children of God. **15** For you didn't receive the spirit of bondage again to fear, but you received the **Spirit of adoption, by whom we cry, "Abba! Father!" 16 The Spirit himself testifies with our spirit that we are children of God**; **17** and if children, then heirs—heirs of God and joint heirs with Christ, if indeed we suffer with him, that we may also be glorified with him.

NOTE: The phrase "strangers who live as foreigners among them" in Hebrew "Ger gur tavek" is a sequence that only appears five times in the Hebrew Bible, with **four** of them occurring in this pairing! (See also Leviticus 18:26). It speaks of those who are not "of Israel" but reside with Israel physically and spiritually. James speaks of his idea in Acts 15:19-20 proposing the four prohibitions of Gentile believers in Christ based on these five mentions. Paul, who was present at that event, now, when writing the Roman church, echoes these four phrases with some of his most famous verses here in Romans 8:15-16. Paul sees this as nothing less than our spiritual adoption by God as His children!

NOTE: This pairing concludes the prior sequences of the word "atonement" (Leviticus 17:11) being echoed by the word "spirit" (Romans 8:14-15). For more, see the notes below the pairing of Leviticus 16:9.

Leviticus 18	Romans 8:18
Lev 18:1 Yahweh spoke to Moses, saying, **2** "Speak to the children of Israel, and say to them, 'I am Yahweh your God. **3** You shall not do as they do in the **land of Egypt**, where you lived. You shall not do as they do in the land of Canaan, where I am bringing you. You shall not follow their statutes. **4** You shall do my ordinances. You shall keep my statutes and follow them. I am Yahweh your God.	**Rom 8:18** For I consider that the **sufferings** of this present time are not worthy to be compared with the glory which will be revealed toward us.

NOTE: The sufferings of the children of Israel in the land of Egypt was not worthy to be compared to the glory that was revealed to them when God appeared to them at Mount Sinai.

Lev 18:5 You shall therefore keep my statutes and my ordinances, which if a man does, he shall live in them. I am Yahweh.

6 "'None of you shall approach anyone who are his close relatives, to uncover their nakedness: I am Yahweh. **7** "'You shall not uncover the nakedness of your father, nor the nakedness of your mother: she is your mother. You shall not uncover her nakedness. **8** "'You shall not uncover the nakedness of your father's wife. It is your father's nakedness. **9** "'You shall not uncover the nakedness of your sister, your father's daughter, or your mother's daughter, whether born at home or born abroad. **10** "'**You shall not uncover the nakedness of your son's daughter, or of your daughter's daughter, even their nakedness; for theirs is your own nakedness**. **11** "'You shall not uncover the nakedness of your father's wife's daughter, conceived by your father, since she is your sister. **12** "'You shall not uncover the nakedness of your father's sister. She is your father's near kinswoman. **13** "'You shall not uncover the nakedness of your mother's sister, for she is your mother's near kinswoman. **14** "'You shall not uncover the nakedness of your father's brother. You shall not approach his wife. She is your aunt. **15** "'You shall not uncover the nakedness of your daughter-in-law. She is your son's wife. You shall not uncover her nakedness. **16** "'You shall not uncover the nakedness of your brother's wife. It is your brother's nakedness. **17** "'You shall not uncover the nakedness of a woman and her daughter. You shall not take her son's daughter, or her daughter's daughter, to uncover her nakedness. They are near kinswomen. **It is wickedness**. **18** You shall not take a wife in addition to her sister, to be a rival, to uncover her nakedness, while her sister is still alive.

19 "'You shall not approach a woman to uncover her nakedness, as long as she is impure by her uncleanness. **20** "'You shall not lie carnally with your neighbor's wife, to defile yourself with her. **21** "'**You shall not give any of your children to sacrifice to Molech**. You shall not profane the name of your God. I am Yahweh. **22** "'You shall not lie with a man as with a woman. That is detestable. **23** "'You shall not lie with any animal to defile yourself with it. Neither shall any woman give herself to an animal, to lie with it: it is a perversion.

Rom 8:19 For the creation waits with eager expectation **for the children of God to be revealed**. 20 For the creation was subjected to vanity, not of its own will, but because of him who subjected it, in hope 21 that the creation itself also will be delivered from the **bondage of decay** into the liberty of the glory of the children of God. 22 For we know that **the whole creation groans and travails in pain together until now**.

NOTE: The idea that the "creation waits in eager expectation for the children of God to be revealed" may seem to be a curious echo for the stern prohibitions of uncovering the nakedness of ones relatives. However, we must remember that from the beginning, this was not so. In the Garden of Eden, it was God's plan at everyone should be "naked an unashamed (Genesis 2:25). It is this return to the fullness of God's original purposes for which all creation eagerly awaits.

Lev 18:24 "'Don't defile yourselves in any of these things; for in all these the nations which I am casting out before you were defiled. **25** The land was defiled. Therefore, I punished its iniquity, and the land vomited out her inhabitants. **26 You therefore shall keep my statutes and my ordinances, and shall not do any of these abominations**; neither the native-born, nor the **stranger who lives as a foreigner among you 27** (for all these abominations have the men of the land done, that were before you, and the land became defiled), **28** lest the land vomit you out also, when you defile it, as it vomited out the nation that was before you. **29** "'For whoever shall do any of these abominations, even the souls that do them shall be cut off from among their people. **30 Therefore you shall keep my requirements**, that you do not practice any of these abominable customs which were practiced before you, and that you do not defile yourselves with them. **I am Yahweh your God**.'"

Rom 8:23 Not only so, but ourselves also, who have the **first fruits of the Spirit**, even we ourselves groan within ourselves, **waiting for adoption**, the redemption of our body. **24** For we were **saved in hope** but hope that is seen is not hope. For who hopes for that which he sees? **25** But if **we hope for that which we don't see**, we wait for it with patience.

NOTE: [Acharei Mot ends.] In this the fifth and final use of the phrase "stranger who lives as a foreigner among you," Paul once again returns to the theme of adoption. (See the notes below Leviticus 17:8)

Leviticus 19

Romans 8:26

Lev 19:1 Yahweh spoke to Moses, saying, **2** "Speak to all the congregation of the children of Israel, and tell them, '**You shall be holy**; for I, **Yahweh your God, am holy**. **3** "'Each one of you shall respect his mother and his father. You shall keep my Sabbaths. I am Yahweh your God. **4** "'Don't turn to idols, nor make **molten gods** for yourselves. I am Yahweh your God.

Rom 8:26 In the same way, **the Spirit** also helps our weaknesses, for we don't know how to pray as we ought. But the Spirit himself makes intercession for us with groanings which can't be uttered. **27** He who searches the hearts knows what is on the Spirit's mind, because he makes intercession for the **saints** according to God.

28 We know that all things work together for good for those who love God, for those who are **called according to his purpose**. **29** For whom he foreknew, he also predestined to be conformed to the **image** of his Son, that he might be the firstborn among many brothers. **30** Whom he predestined, those he also called. Whom he called, those he also justified. Whom he justified, those he also glorified.

NOTE: [Kedoshim.] The reason that all things work together for good to those who love God, for those who are "called according to his purpose," is that God's purpose is that we shall be holy because He, our God, is holy. Simply put, God's purpose for us is **our holiness** together with himself. Concerning the last echo, The Hebrew word for "molten gods" can also be translated as "image."

Lev 19:5 "'**When you offer a sacrifice of peace offerings to Yahweh, you shall offer it so that you may be accepted**. **6** It shall be eaten the same day you offer it, and on the next day. If anything remains until the third day, it shall be burned with fire. **7** If it is eaten at all on the third day, it is an abomination. It will not **be accepted**; **8** but everyone who eats it shall bear his iniquity, because he has profaned the holy thing of Yahweh, and that soul shall be **cut off** from his people.

Rom 8:31 What then shall we say about these things? If God is for us, who can be against us? **32 He who didn't spare his own Son, but delivered him up for us all, how would he not also with him freely give us all things**? **33** Who could bring a charge against God's chosen ones? **It is God who justifies**. **34** Who is he who condemns? It is Christ who died, yes rather, who was raised from the dead, who is at the right hand of God, who also makes intercession for us. **35** Who shall **separate us** from the love of Christ? Could oppression, or anguish, or persecution, or famine, or nakedness, or peril, or sword? **36** Even as it is written, "For your sake we are killed all day long. We were accounted as sheep for the slaughter."

Lev 19:9 "'When you **reap the harvest of your land**, you shall not wholly reap the corners of your field, neither shall you gather the gleanings of your harvest. **10** You shall not glean your vineyard, neither shall you gather the fallen grapes of your vineyard. You shall **leave them for the poor and for the foreigner**. I am **Yahweh your God**.

Rom 8:37 No, in all these things we are **more than conquerors** through him who loved us. **38** For I am persuaded that neither death, nor life, nor angels, nor principalities, nor things present, nor things to come, nor powers, **39** nor height, nor depth, nor any other created thing will be able to **separate us from God's love** which is in **Christ Jesus our Lord**.

NOTE: The command not to fully reap the harvest but always leave something for the poor and the foreigner is considered one of the most loving of all the commandments. Paul echoes this with some of the most beautiful words of the entire New Testament, assuring us of the extent of God's desire for us to be joined with him. The phrase "more than conquerors" also beautifully echoes the Leviticus 19:9's assurance to the children of Israel that yes, they would take possession of the Promised Land, but not in a way that excludes anyone who desires to live peacefully among them.

Leviticus 19:11   Romans 9

Lev 19:11 "'You shall not steal. "'**You shall not lie**. "'You shall not deceive one another. **12** "'You shall not **swear** by my name falsely and profane the **name of your God**. I am Yahweh. **13** "'You shall not **oppress** your neighbor, nor rob him. "'The wages of a hired servant shall not remain with you all night until the morning. **14** "'You shall not **curse** the deaf, nor put a stumbling block before the blind; but you shall fear your God. I am Yahweh. **15** "'You shall do no injustice in judgment. You shall not be partial to the poor, nor show favoritism to the great; but you shall judge your neighbor in righteousness. **16** "'You shall not go around as a slanderer **among your people**. "'You shall not endanger the life of your neighbor. I am **Yahweh**.

Rom 9:1 I tell the truth in Christ. **I am not lying**, my conscience **testifying** with me in the **Holy Spirit 2** that I have great sorrow and **unceasing pain** in my heart. **3** For I could wish that I myself were **accursed** from Christ for my brothers' sake, my kinsmen according to the flesh **4** who are Israelites; whose is the adoption, the glory, the covenants, the giving of the law, the service, and the promises; **5** whose are the fathers, and **from whom is Christ as concerning the flesh**, who is over all, **God**, blessed forever. Amen.

NOTE: The abrupt shift in tone at this point in both Leviticus and Romans is startling.

Lev 19:17 "'You shall not hate your brother in your heart. **You shall surely rebuke your neighbor** and not bear sin because of him. **18** "'You shall not take vengeance, nor bear any grudge against the **children of your people**; but you shall love your neighbor as yourself. I am Yahweh. **19** "'You shall keep my statutes. "'You shall not crossbreed different kinds of animals. "'You shall not sow your field with two kinds of seed; "'**Don't wear a garment made of two kinds of material**.

Rom 9:6 But it is not as though the word of God has come to nothing. For **they are not all Israel** that are of Israel. **7** Neither, because they are **Abraham's offspring, are they all children**. But "your offspring will be accounted as from Isaac." **8** That is, it is not the children of the flesh who are children of God, but the children of the promise are counted as heirs. **9** For this is a word of promise: "At the appointed time I will come, and Sarah will have a son." **10** Not only so, but Rebecca also conceived by one, by our father Isaac. **11** For being not yet born, neither having done anything good or bad, that the purpose of God according to election might stand, not of works, but of him who calls, **12** it was said to her, "The elder will serve the younger." **13** Even as it is written, "**Jacob I loved, but Esau I hated**."

NOTE: One of the most debated sentences from Paul is the meaning of "For they are not all Israel that are of Israel." The Leviticus side of this echo affirms that Paul *is intending a strong rebuke*. However, this is moderated by the word "neighbor" which is also regularly translated as "brother" (*ach* in Hebrew). However, one might interpret Paul's meaning in Romans 9:6-7, the echo hints that we should be careful not to enter into sin or bear any grudge against those *ach* (brothers) who we might place in the group "they are not all Israel." The word "children" in Lev. 19:18 is also translated "sons" (*ben* in Hebrew).

NOTE: Concerning the echo of a garment made of two kinds of material, and Jacob/Esau, one interpretation is this. While God loved Esau as an individual, Esau and the people that descended from him voluntarily chose to live outside the land of Israel in what became Edom, whereas Jacob returned as soon as he was able. God did not force Jacob (eventually Israel) to join himself with Esau (eventually Edom) and try to build from these two very different "materials" a single nation. It is not as if God loves one kind of material and hates the other, but rather the distinction between them is impossible to join together as one. Instead, God waits for the sojourners who are willing to sojourn in the midst of Israel, (see note on Lev. 17:8) to build his garment of praise (Isaiah 61:3).

Lev 19:20 "'If a man lies **carnally** with a woman who is a slave girl, pledged to be married to another man, and not yet redeemed or given her freedom; they shall be punished. **They shall not be put to death, because she was not free**. 21 He shall bring his trespass offering to Yahweh, to the door of the Tent of Meeting, even a ram for a trespass offering. **22** The priest shall make atonement for him with the ram of the trespass offering before Yahweh for his sin which he has committed; and **the sin which he has committed shall be forgiven him**. **23** "'When you come into the land, and have planted all kinds of trees for food, then you shall count their fruit as forbidden. For three years it shall be forbidden to you. It shall not be eaten. **24** But in the fourth year all its fruit shall be holy, for giving praise to Yahweh. **25** In the fifth year you shall eat its fruit, that it may yield its increase to you. I am Yahweh your God.

Rom 9:14 What shall we say then? Is there **unrighteousness** with God? May it never be! **15** For he said to Moses, "I will have mercy on whom I have mercy, and **I will have compassion on whom I have compassion**." **16** So then it is not of him who wills, nor of him who runs, but of **God who has mercy**. **17** For the Scripture says to Pharaoh, "For this very purpose I caused you to be raised up, that I might show in you my power, and that my name might be proclaimed in all the earth." **18** So then, he has mercy on whom he desires, and he hardens whom he desires.

Lev 19:26 "'You shall not eat any meat with the blood still in it. You shall not use enchantments, nor practice sorcery. **27** "'You shall not cut the hair on the sides of your head or clip off the edge of your beard. **28** "'You shall not make any cuttings in your flesh for the dead, nor tattoo any marks on yourself. **I am Yahweh**. **29** "'Don't profane your daughter, to make her a prostitute; lest the land fall to prostitution, and the land become full of wickedness. **30** "'You shall keep my Sabbaths and reverence **my sanctuary**; I am Yahweh. **31** "'Don't turn to those who are mediums, nor to the wizards. Don't seek them out, to be defiled by them. I am Yahweh your God. **32** "'You shall rise up before the gray head and **honor** the face of the elderly, and you shall fear your God. I am Yahweh.

33 "'If a foreigner lives as a foreigner with you in your land, you shall not do him wrong. **34 The foreigner who lives as a foreigner with you shall be to you as the native-born among you**, and you shall love him as yourself; for **you lived as foreigners in the land of Egypt**. I am Yahweh your God.

35 "'You shall do no unrighteousness in judgment, in measures of length, of weight, or of quantity. **36** You shall have just balances, just weights, a just ephah, and a just hin. I am **Yahweh your God, who brought you out of the land of Egypt**. **37** "'You shall observe all my statutes and all my ordinances and do them. I am Yahweh.'"

Rom 9:19 You will say then to me, "Why does he still find fault? **For who withstands his will**?" **20** But indeed, O man, who are you to reply against God? **Will the thing formed ask him who formed it**, "Why did you make me like this?" **21** Or hasn't the potter a right over the clay, from the same lump to make one part a vessel for **honor**, and another for dishonor? **22** What if God, willing to show his wrath and to make his power known, endured with much patience vessels of wrath prepared for destruction, **23** and that he might make known the riches of his glory on vessels of mercy, which he prepared beforehand for glory— **24 us, whom he also called, not from the Jews only, but also from the Gentiles**? **25** As he says also in Hosea, "**I will call them 'my people,' which were not my people**; and her 'beloved,' who was not beloved." **26** "It will be that in the place where it was said to them, 'You are not my people,' there they will be called '**children of the living God**.'"

NOTE: The Sabbath and the sanctuary were specifically *formed* by God.

Leviticus 20   Romans 9:27

Lev 20:1 Yahweh spoke to Moses, saying, **2** "Moreover, you shall tell the children of Israel, 'Anyone of the **children of Israel**, or of the strangers who live as foreigners in Israel, who gives any of his offspring to Molech shall surely be put to death. The people of the land shall stone him with stones. **3** I also will set my face against that person, and will **cut him off** from among his people, because he has given of his offspring to Molech, to defile my sanctuary and to profane my holy name. **4** If the people of the land all hide their eyes from that person when he gives of his offspring to Molech, and don't put him to death, **5** then I will set my face against that man and against his family, and will cut him off, and all who play the prostitute after him to play the prostitute with Molech, from among their people. **6** "'The person that turns to those who are mediums and wizards, to play the prostitute after them, I will even set my face against that person and **will cut him off from among his people**. **7** "'Sanctify yourselves therefore and be holy; for I am Yahweh your God. **8** You shall keep my statutes and do them. I am Yahweh who sanctifies you.

Rom 9:27 Isaiah cries concerning Israel, "If the number of the **children of Israel** are as the sand of the sea, it is the remnant who will be saved; **28** for he will finish the work and **cut it short** in righteousness, because the Lord will make a short work upon the earth." **29a** As Isaiah has said before, "**Unless the Lord of Armies had left us a seed**,

NOTE: In this pairing we find in Romans the promise of the continuation of the faithful remnant in Israel and we see in Leviticus the prohibition of occult sacrifices, and that any person who partakes in them is to be cut off, some even to the point of death (Lev. 20:2).

Lev 20:9 "'For everyone who curses his father or his mother shall surely be put to death. He has cursed his father or his mother. His blood shall be upon himself.

10 "'The man who commits adultery with another man's wife, even he who commits adultery with his neighbor's wife, the adulterer and the adulteress shall surely be put to death. **11** "'The man who lies with his father's wife has uncovered his father's nakedness. Both of them shall surely be put to death. Their blood shall be upon themselves. **12** "'If a man lies with his daughter-in-law, both of them shall surely be put to death. They have committed a perversion. Their blood shall be upon themselves. **13** "'**If a man lies with a male, as he lies with a woman, both of them have committed an abomination**. They shall surely be put to death. Their blood shall be upon themselves. **14** "'If a man takes a wife and her mother, it is wickedness. They shall be burned with fire, both he and they, that there may be no wickedness among you. **15** "'If a man lies with an animal, he shall surely be put to death; and you shall kill the animal. **16** "'If a woman approaches any animal and lies with it, you shall kill the woman and the animal. They shall surely be put to death. Their blood shall be upon themselves.

17 "'If a man takes his sister, his father's daughter, or his mother's daughter, and sees her nakedness, and she sees his nakedness, it is a shameful thing. **They shall be cut off in the sight of the children of their people**. He has uncovered his sister's nakedness. He shall bear his iniquity. **18** "'If a man lies with a woman having her monthly period, and uncovers her nakedness, he has made naked her fountain, and she has uncovered the fountain of her blood. Both of them shall be cut off from among their people. **19** "'You shall not uncover the nakedness of your mother's sister, nor of your father's sister, for he has made his close relative naked. They shall bear their iniquity. **20** If a man lies with his uncle's wife, he has uncovered his uncle's nakedness. They shall bear their sin. They shall die childless. **21** "'If a man takes his brother's wife, it is an impurity. He has uncovered his brother's nakedness. They shall **be childless**.

Rom 9:29b would have become like **Sodom** and would have been made like Gomorrah."

30 What shall we say then? That the Gentiles, who didn't follow after righteousness, attained to righteousness, even the righteousness which is of faith; **31** but **Israel, following after a law of righteousness, didn't arrive at the law of righteousness**. **32** Why? Because they didn't seek it by faith, but as it were by works of the law. They stumbled over the stumbling stone, **33** even as it is written, "Behold, I lay in Zion a stumbling stone and a rock of offense; and no one who believes in him will **be disappointed**."

Leviticus 20:22	**Romans 10**
Lev 20:22 "'You shall therefore keep all my statutes and all my ordinances, and do them, that **the land where I am bringing you to dwell** may not vomit you out. 23 You shall not walk in the customs of the nation which I am casting out before you; for **they did all these things**, and **therefore I abhorred them**. 24 But I have said to you, "You shall inherit their land, and I will give it to you to possess it, a land flowing with milk and honey." **I am Yahweh your God, who has separated you from the peoples**. 25 "'You shall therefore **make a distinction between** the clean animal and the unclean, and between the unclean <u>bird</u> and the clean. You shall not make yourselves abominable by animal, or by bird, or by anything with which the <u>ground</u> teems, which I have separated from you as unclean for you.	Rom 10:1 Brothers, my heart's desire and my prayer to God is for Israel, **that they may be saved**. 2 For I testify about them that they have a zeal for God, but not according to knowledge. 3 For being ignorant of God's righteousness, and <u>seeking to establish their own righteousness</u>, they didn't subject themselves to **the righteousness of God**. 4 For <u>Christ is the fulfillment of the law for righteousness to everyone who believes</u>. 5 For Moses writes about the righteousness of the law, "The **one who does them** will live by them." 6 But the righteousness which is of faith says this, "Don't say in your heart, 'Who will <u>ascend</u> into heaven?' (that is, to bring Christ down); 7 or, 'Who will <u>descend</u> into the abyss?' (That is, to bring Christ up from the dead.)"

NOTE: Regarding Leviticus 20:25 and Romans 10:6-7, it is possible that the word "ascend" is Paul's echo of "bird" and the word "descend" is an echo of "ground."

Lev 20:26 You shall be holy to me, for I, Yahweh, am holy, and have set you apart from the peoples, **that you should be mine**. 27 "'A man or a woman that is a <u>medium or is a wizard</u> shall surely be put to death. They shall be stoned with stones. **Their blood shall be upon themselves**.'"	Rom 10:8 But what does it say? "The word is near you, in your mouth and in your heart;" that is, the word of faith which we preach: 9 that if you will confess with your mouth that Jesus is Lord and believe in your heart that God raised him from the dead, **you will be saved**. 10 For with the heart one believes resulting in righteousness; and with the mouth confession is made resulting in salvation. 11 For the Scripture says, "Whoever believes in him will not be **disappointed**." 12 For there is no distinction between Jew and Greek; for the same Lord is Lord of all and is rich to all who call on him. 13 For, "**Whoever will call on the name of the Lord will be saved**."

NOTE: [Kedoshim ends.] In Romans 10:11, the belief in the power of the risen Lord Jesus is contrasted with the belief in persons who engage in the occult. In Rom. 10:13, "Whoever will call on the name of the Lord shall be saved" is contrasted with those whose "blood shall be upon themselves" in their death.

Leviticus 21

Romans 10:14

Lev 21:1 Yahweh said to Moses, "Speak to the priests, the sons of Aaron, and say to them, 'A priest shall not defile himself for **the dead among his people**, 2 except for his <u>relatives that are near to him</u>: for his mother, for his father, for his son, for his daughter, for his brother, 3 and for his virgin sister who is near to him, who has had no husband; for her he may defile himself. **4** He shall not defile himself, being a chief man among his people, to profane himself. **5** "'They shall not shave their heads or shave off the corners of their beards or make any cuttings in their flesh. **6** They shall be **holy** to their God, and not profane the name of their God, for they offer the offerings of Yahweh made by fire, **the bread of their God**. Therefore, they shall be holy. **7** "'They shall not marry a woman who is a prostitute, or profane. A priest shall not marry a woman divorced from her husband; for he is holy to his God. **8** You shall sanctify him therefore, for **he offers the bread of your God**. He shall be holy to you, for I Yahweh, who sanctify you, am holy. **9** "'The daughter of any priest, if she profanes herself by playing the prostitute, she profanes her father. She shall be burned with fire.

Rom 10:14 How then will they call on him in whom **they have not believed**? How will they believe in him whom **they have not heard**? How will they hear without a preacher? **15** And how will they preach unless they are sent? As it is written: "How beautiful are the **feet** of those who preach the Good News of peace, **who bring glad tidings of good things!**"

16 But they didn't all listen to the glad news. For Isaiah says, "Lord, who has believed our report?" **17 So faith comes by hearing, and hearing by the word of God.**

18 But I say, didn't they hear? Yes, most certainly, "Their sound went out into all the earth, their words to the ends of the world."

NOTE: [Emor.] The word "holy" in Leviticus 20:6 is proposed to echo the "feet" of those holy ones who preach the Good News. More specifically, Moses was told to remove his sandals from his feet, because he was standing on holy ground (Exodus 3:5). The proposed echo between Leviticus 21:8 and Romans 10:17 is based on Matthew 4:4.

Lev 21:10 "'**He who is the high priest among his brothers, on whose head the anointing oil is poured**, and who is consecrated to put on the garments, shall not let the hair of his head hang loose, or tear his clothes. **11** He shall not go into any dead body or defile himself for his father or for his mother. **12** He shall not go out of the sanctuary, nor profane the sanctuary of his God; for the crown of the anointing oil of his God is on him. I am Yahweh. **13** "'**He shall take a wife in her virginity**. **14** He shall not marry a widow, or one divorced, or a woman who has been defiled, or a prostitute. **He shall take** a virgin of his own people as a wife. **15** He shall not **profane his offspring among his people**, for I am Yahweh who sanctifies him.'"

Rom 10:19 But I ask, **didn't Israel know**? First Moses says, "I will provoke you to jealousy with that which is no nation. I will make you angry with a nation void of understanding." **20** Isaiah is very bold and says, "**I was found by those who didn't seek me**. I was revealed to those who didn't ask for me." **21** But about Israel he says, "All day long **I stretched** out my hands to a **disobedient and contrary people**."

NOTE: The high priest had positioning, knowledge and special anointing. If the high priest does not know God's plans for the nation of Israel, who would know? (See Matthew 26:65 for *not knowing*, and John 11:50 for *knowing*.) Concerning the echo of "I stretched" with "He shall take", a person "takes" something by stretching out his hands.

Leviticus 21:16

Romans 11

Lev 21:16 Yahweh spoke to Moses, saying, **17** "Tell Aaron, 'None of your **offspring throughout their generations** who has a defect **may approach** to offer the bread of his God. **18** For whatever man he is that has a defect, he shall not approach: a **blind** man, or a lame, or he who has a flat nose, or any deformity, **19** or a man who has an injured foot, or an injured hand, **20** or hunchbacked, or a dwarf, **or one who has a defect in his eye**, or an itching disease, or scabs, or who has damaged testicles.

Rom 11:1 I ask then, did God reject his people? May it never be! For I also am an Israelite, **a descendant of Abraham, of the tribe of Benjamin**. **2** God didn't reject his people, whom he foreknew. Or don't you know what the Scripture says about Elijah? How he **pleads with God** against Israel: **3** "Lord, they have killed your prophets, they have broken down your altars. I am left alone, and they seek my life." **4** But how does God answer him? "I have reserved for myself seven thousand men who have not bowed the knee to Baal." **5** Even so too at this present time also there is a remnant according to the election of grace. **6** And if by grace, then it is no longer of works; otherwise, grace is no longer grace. But if it is of works, it is no longer grace; otherwise, work is no longer work.

7 What then? That which Israel seeks for, that he didn't obtain, but the chosen ones obtained it, and the rest were hardened. **8** According as it is written, "God gave them a spirit of stupor, **eyes that they should not see**, and ears that they should not hear, to this very day." **9** David says, "Let their table be made a snare, a trap, a stumbling block, and a retribution to them. **10 Let their eyes be darkened, that they may not see**. Always keep their backs bent."

Lev 21:21 No man of the offspring of Aaron the priest who has a defect shall come near to offer the offerings of Yahweh made by fire. **Since he has a defect, he shall not come near to offer the bread of his God**. **22** He shall **eat the bread** of his God, both of the most holy, and of the holy. **23** He shall not come near to the veil, nor come near to the altar, because he has a defect; that he may not profane my sanctuaries, for I am **Yahweh who sanctifies them**.'" **24** So **Moses** spoke to Aaron, and to his **sons**, and to all the **children of Israel**.

Rom 11:11 I ask then, did they stumble that they might fall? May it never be! **But by their fall salvation has come to the Gentiles**, to provoke them to jealousy. **12** Now if their fall is the riches of the world, and their loss the riches of the Gentiles, how much more **their fullness**? **13** For I speak to you who are Gentiles. Since then, I am an apostle to Gentiles, I glorify my ministry, **14** if by any means I may provoke to jealousy those who are my flesh and may save some of them. **15** For if the rejection of them is the reconciling of the world, **what would their acceptance be**, but **life from the dead**? **16** If the first fruit is holy, so is the lump. If the **root** is holy, so are the **branches**.

NOTE: "Moses" echoes "life from the dead" in the account of Christ's transfiguration. In the last two echoes: "root" and "branches" Paul likely sees a correspondence. To the Roman church, Paul writes that the Jews are the *root* and the Gentiles are the *branches*, but in the Leviticus passage and within the Jewish world, the children of Israel are like the branches and the Levities (especially the priests – the sons of Aaron) are like the root, in the sense that it was through the Levites that the Law was brought forth to all the people.

Leviticus 22	Romans 11:17

Lev 22:1 Yahweh spoke to Moses, saying, **2** "Tell Aaron and his sons **to separate themselves from the holy things of the children of Israel**, which **they make holy** to me, and **that they not profane** my holy name. I am Yahweh. **3** Tell them, 'If anyone of all your **offspring** throughout your generations approaches the holy things which the children of Israel **make holy** to Yahweh, having his uncleanness on him, **that soul shall be cut off from before me**. I am Yahweh.

Rom 11:17 But if <u>some of the branches were broken off</u>, and you, being a wild olive, were **grafted in among them** and became **partaker with them** of the root and of the richness of the olive tree, **18** don't boast over the **branches**. But if you boast, remember that it is not you who support the root, but the root supports you. **19** You will say then, "Branches were broken off, that I might be grafted in." **20** True; by their unbelief they were broken off, and you stand by your faith. Don't be conceited, but <u>fear</u>; **21** for **if God didn't spare the natural branches, neither will he spare you**.

NOTE: The phrase "partaker with them" (i.e. with Israel) echoing "that they not profane my holy name" may relate to the fact that God is called "the God of Israel" about 200 times. Paul's word "fear" echoing "make holy" finds support in 2 Corinthians 7:1. The consequences of not fearing God in this matter are found in the next verse, Romans 11:21. Here "neither will he spare you" has often been interpreted as meaning "cut off," exactly what is echoed in Leviticus.

Lev 22:4 "'Whoever of the offspring of Aaron is a leper or has a discharge shall not eat of the holy things until he is clean. Whoever touches anything that is unclean by the dead, or a man who has a seminal emission, **5** or whoever touches any creeping thing whereby he may be made unclean, or a man from whom he may become unclean, whatever uncleanness he has— **6** the person that touches any such shall be unclean until the evening, and **shall not eat of the holy things unless he bathes his body in water**. **7** When the sun is down, **he shall be clean; and afterward he shall eat of the holy things**, because it is his bread. **8** He shall not eat that which dies of itself or is torn by animals, defiling himself by it. I am Yahweh. **9** "'**They shall therefore follow my commandment**, lest they bear sin for it and die in it, if they profane it. **I am Yahweh who sanctifies them**.

Rom 11:22 See then the goodness and severity of God. Toward those who fell, severity; but toward you, goodness, if you continue in his goodness; otherwise, you also will be cut off. **23** They also, **if they don't continue in their unbelief**, will be grafted in, for **God is able to graft them in again**. **24** For if you were cut out of that which is by nature a wild olive tree, and were grafted contrary to nature into a **good olive tree**, how much more will these, which are the natural branches, **be grafted into their own olive tree**?

NOTE: Paul's phrase "if they don't continue in their unbelief" seems to be appropriately echoed in the phrase "unless he bathes his body in water," which is strongly echoed to baptism in Leviticus 14:8-9. Concerning the proposed echo between "God is able to graft them in again" and "he shall be clean; and afterward he shall eat of the holy things," while anyone who touches anything that is unclean, is immediately unclean, the goodness of God is such that their uncleanliness only lasts until the evening. The "good olive tree" echoes "the shall therefore follow my commandment" in that the very first commandment given to mankind was not to eat of the *tree* of knowledge of good and evil.

Lev 22:10 "'No stranger shall eat of the holy thing: a **foreigner living with the priests**, or a hired servant, shall not eat of the holy thing. **11** <u>But if a priest buys a slave, purchased by his money, he shall eat of it; and those who are born in his house shall eat of his bread</u>. **12** If a priest's daughter is married to an outsider, she shall not eat of the heave offering of the holy things. **13** But if a priest's **daughter** is a widow, or divorced, and has no child, and has <u>returned</u> to her **father's** house <u>as in her youth</u>, she may eat of her father's bread; but no stranger shall eat any of it. **14** "'If a man eats something holy unwittingly, then he shall add the fifth part of its value to it and shall give the holy thing to the priest. 15 The priests shall not profane the holy things of the children of Israel, which they offer to Yahweh, **16** and so cause them to bear the **iniquity that brings guilt** when they eat their holy things; for <u>I am Yahweh who sanctifies them</u>.'"

Rom 11:25 For I don't desire you to be ignorant, **brothers, of this mystery**, so that you won't be wise in your own conceits, that a partial hardening has happened to Israel, until the <u>fullness of the Gentiles</u> has come in, **26** and so **all Israel** will **be saved**. Even as it is written, "There will come out of Zion the Deliverer, and he will turn away ungodliness from Jacob. **27** This is my covenant with them, when I will take away their sins." **28** Concerning the Good News, they are enemies for your sake. But concerning the election, they are beloved for the **fathers'** sake. **29** For the gifts and the calling of God are <u>irrevocable</u>. **30** For as you in time past were disobedient to God, but now have obtained mercy by their disobedience, **31** even so these also have now been disobedient, that by the mercy shown to you they may also obtain mercy. **32 For God has bound all to disobedience**, that he might have mercy on all.

33 Oh the depth of the riches both of the wisdom and the knowledge of God! How unsearchable are his judgments, and his ways past tracing out! **34** "For who has known the mind of the Lord? Or who has been his counselor?" **35** "Or who has first given to him, and it will be repaid to him again?" **36** <u>For of him and through him and to him are all things. To him be the glory forever! Amen</u>.

In one of the most fascinating echoes between the two books, Paul sees a mystery in the phrase "if a priest buys a slave". Indeed, it was the Jews who brought the Gentiles into faith through their preaching of the gospel to them and allowing them to be brought into the house of Israel. Now it is the slaves (Gentiles) who have achieved dominance over the priest's daughter who has left the household, but God has not forgotten the daughter's calling, and she will return "as in her youth." Indeed, both the slave and the daughter are guilty before God, and both will be sanctified.

Leviticus 22:17	Romans 12

Lev 22:17 Yahweh spoke to Moses, saying, **18** "**Speak** to Aaron, and to his sons, and to all the children of Israel, and say to them, 'Whoever is of the house of Israel, or of the foreigners in Israel, **who offers his offering, whether it is any of their vows or any of their free will offerings**, which they **offer to Yahweh** for a burnt offering: **19** that you may be accepted, *you shall offer a male without defect, of the bulls, of the sheep, or of the goats*. **20** But you shall not offer anything that has a defect, for it shall not be acceptable for you. **21** Whoever offers a sacrifice of peace offerings to Yahweh to accomplish a vow, or for a free will offering of the herd or of the flock, it shall be **perfect to be accepted**. There shall be **no defect in it**. **22** You shall not offer what is blind, or injured, or maimed, or has a wart, or is festering, or has a running sore to Yahweh, nor make an offering by fire of them on the altar to Yahweh. **23** Either **a bull or a lamb** that has any deformity or lacking in his parts, that you may offer for a free will offering; but for a vow it shall not be accepted. **24** You shall not offer to Yahweh that which has its testicles bruised, crushed, broken, or cut. You shall not do this in your land. **25** You shall not offer any of these as the bread of your God from the hand of a foreigner, because their corruption is in them. There is a defect in them. They shall not be accepted for you.'"

26 Yahweh spoke to Moses, saying, **27** "When a bull, a sheep, or a goat is born, it shall remain seven days with its mother. From the eighth day on it shall be accepted for the offering of an offering made by fire to Yahweh. **28** Whether it is a cow or ewe, you shall not kill it and its young both in one day.

Rom 12:1 Therefore I **urge** you, brothers, by the mercies of God, to **present your bodies a living sacrifice**, holy, acceptable to God, which is your **spiritual service**. 2 Don't be conformed to this world, but be transformed by the renewing of your mind, so that you may prove what is the *good, well-pleasing, and perfect will of God*.

3 For I say through the grace that was given me, to everyone who is among you, **not to think of himself more highly than he ought to think**; but to **think reasonably**, as God has apportioned to each person a measure of faith. 4 For even as we have many members in one body, and all the members don't have the same function, 5 so we, who are many, are one body in Christ, and individually members of one another, 6 having **gifts differing** according to the grace that was given to us: if prophecy, let's prophesy according to the proportion of our faith; 7 or service, let's give ourselves to service; or he who teaches, to his teaching; 8 or he who exhorts, to his exhorting; he who gives, let him do it with generosity; he who rules, with diligence; he who shows mercy, with cheerfulness.

NOTE: "Good, well-pleasing and perfect" echoes "bulls, sheep and goats." In Leviticus 22:23, Bulls and lambs echo "having gifts differing." This sectional pairing ends with the seven redemptive gifts: prophecy thru mercy, echoing the reasons an offering cannot be accepted (these seven are underlined but not bolded). A possible reason for the seven-fold correspondence is as follows: might each type of deformity represent a "type of problem" that each differing gift is best suited to mend?

Lev 22:29 "'When you sacrifice a sacrifice of thanksgiving to Yahweh, you shall sacrifice it so that you may be accepted. **30** It shall be **eaten on the same day**; you shall **leave none of it until the morning**. I am Yahweh. **31** "'**Therefore you shall keep my commandments** and do them. I am Yahweh.

Rom 12:9 Let love be without hypocrisy. Abhor that which is evil. Cling to that which is good. **10** In love of the brothers be tenderly affectionate to one another; in honor prefer one another, **11 not lagging** in diligence, **fervent in spirit**, serving the Lord, **12** rejoicing in hope, enduring in troubles, continuing steadfastly in prayer, **13** contributing to the needs of the saints, and given to hospitality.

14 Bless those who persecute you; bless, and don't curse. **15** Rejoice with those who rejoice. Weep with those who weep. **16** Be of the same mind one toward another. Don't set your mind on high things but associate with the humble. Don't be wise in your own conceits. **17** Repay no one evil for evil. Respect what is honorable in the sight of all men. **18** If it is possible, as much as it is up to you, be at peace with all men. **19** Don't seek revenge yourselves, beloved, but give place to God's wrath. For it is written, "Vengeance belongs to me; I will repay, says the Lord." **20** Therefore "If your enemy is hungry, feed him. If he is thirsty, give him a drink; for in doing so, you will heap coals of fire on his head." **21** Don't be overcome by evil, but overcome evil with good.

NOTE: Paul's phrase "not lagging" echoes "eaten on the same day" as both phrases involve a judicious sense of time. "Fervent" (*zeo* in Greek) means "to be hot," which applies readily to the phrase "leave none of it until the morning." Romans 12:14 is strongly reminiscent of Jesus's commands in Matthew 5:44 and Luke 6:28, echoing Leviticus.

Lev. 22:32	Romans 13

Lev 22:32 You shall not profane my holy name, but **I will be made holy among the children of Israel**. I am Yahweh who makes you holy, **33** who **brought you out of the land of Egypt, to be your God**. I am Yahweh."

Rom 13:1 Let every soul be in subjection to the higher authorities, <u>**for there is no authority except from God, and those who exist are ordained by God**</u>. **2** Therefore he who resists the authority withstands the ordinance of God; and those who withstand will receive to themselves judgment. **3** For rulers are not a terror to the good work, but to the evil. Do you desire to have no fear of the authority? Do that which is good, and you will have praise from the authority, **4** for he is a servant of God to you for good. But if you do that which is evil, be afraid, for he doesn't bear the sword in vain; for he is a servant of God, an avenger for wrath to him who does evil. **5** Therefore you need to be in subjection, not only because of the wrath, but also for conscience' sake. **6** For this reason you also pay taxes, for they are servants of God's service, continually doing this very thing. **7** Therefore give everyone what you owe: taxes to whom taxes are due; customs to whom customs; respect to whom respect; honor to whom honor.

8 Owe no one anything, except to love one another; for he who loves his neighbor has fulfilled the law. **9** For this, "**You shall not commit adultery,**" "**You shall not murder,**" "**You shall not steal,**" "**You shall not covet,**" **and whatever other commandments there are**, are all summed up in this saying, namely, "You shall love your neighbor as yourself." **10** Love doesn't harm a neighbor. Love therefore is the fulfillment of the law.

NOTE: The first echo suggests that a nation's holiness is still lacking unless it sees in its leaders an authority given from God. The list of commandments in Romans 13:9 was given to the people a mere fifty days after the people were brought up out of the land of Egypt.

Leviticus 23	Romans 13:11
Lev 23:1 Yahweh spoke to Moses, saying, **2** "Speak to the children of Israel, and tell them, 'The **set feasts** of Yahweh, which you shall proclaim to be holy convocations, even these are my **set feasts**. **3** "'**Six days** shall work be done, but on the seventh day is a Sabbath of solemn rest, a holy convocation; you shall do no kind of work. It is a **Sabbath to Yahweh** in all your dwellings.	**Rom 13:11** Do this, knowing the **time**, that it is already **time** for you to awaken out of sleep, for salvation is now nearer to us than when we first believed. **12** The night is far gone, and the day is near. Let's therefore throw off the deeds of darkness, and let's put on the armor of light. **13** **Let's walk properly, as in the day;** not in reveling and drunkenness, not in sexual promiscuity and lustful acts, and not in strife and jealousy. **14** But put on the **Lord Jesus Christ, and make no provision** for the flesh, for its lusts.

NOTE: Paul is about to talk about days and foods but makes a few brief mentions regarding time. He seems to stress *how we can walk properly* during the six days, and regarding Sabbath, his echo of concern seems centered on not *making* provision for the flesh and its lusts. Said another way, Paul seems to be much less concerned about how the Gentile and Jewish believers in Rome might differ in their treatment of "*make* no fire" in Exodus 35:3 but would instead emphatically exhort Jew and Gentile alike that whatever they do or do not do on Shabbat they must "*make* no provision for sinful lusts."

Leviticus 23:4	Romans 14

Lev 23:4 "'These are the set feasts of Yahweh, even holy convocations, which you shall proclaim in their appointed season. **5** In the first month, on the fourteenth day of the month in the evening, is Yahweh's Passover. **6** On the fifteenth day of the same month is the feast of unleavened bread to Yahweh. Seven days you shall **eat unleavened bread**. **7** In the first day you shall have a holy convocation. You shall do no regular work. **8** But you shall offer an offering made by fire to Yahweh seven days. In the seventh day is a holy convocation. You shall do no regular work.'"

9 Yahweh spoke to Moses, saying, **10** "Speak to the children of Israel, and tell them, 'When you have come into the land which I give to you, and shall reap its harvest, then **you shall bring the sheaf of the first fruits** of your harvest to the priest. **11** He shall wave the sheaf before Yahweh, to **be accepted for you**. On the next day after the Sabbath the priest shall wave it. **12** On the day when you wave the sheaf, **you shall offer a male lamb without defect a year old** for a burnt offering to Yahweh.

Rom 14:1 Now accept one who is weak in faith, but not for disputes over opinions. **2** One man has faith to **eat all things**, but he who is weak eats only vegetables. **3 Don't let him who eats despise him who doesn't eat**. Don't let him who doesn't eat judge him who eats, **for God has accepted him**. **4** Who are you who judge another's servant? **To his own lord he stands or falls**. Yes, he will be made to stand, for God has power to make him stand.

Lev 23:13 The meal offering with it shall be two tenths of an ephah of fine flour mixed with oil, an offering made by fire to Yahweh for a pleasant aroma; and the drink offering with it shall be of wine, the fourth part of a hin. **14 You shall eat no bread, no roasted grain, and no green ears, until this same day, until you have brought the offering of your God**. This is a statute forever throughout your generations in all your dwellings.

15 "You shall count from the next day after the Sabbath, from the day that you brought the sheaf of the wave offering: seven Sabbaths shall be completed. **16** The next day after the seventh Sabbath you shall count fifty days; and you shall offer a new meal offering to Yahweh. **17 You shall bring out of your habitations two loaves of bread** for a wave offering made of two tenths of an ephah of fine flour. They shall be baked with yeast, for first fruits to Yahweh. **18** You shall present with the bread seven lambs without defect a year old, one young bull, and two rams. They shall be a burnt offering to Yahweh, with their meal offering and their drink offerings, an offering made by fire, of a sweet aroma to Yahweh. **19** You shall offer one male goat for a sin offering, and two male lambs a year old for a sacrifice of peace offerings. **20** The priest shall wave them with the bread of the first fruits for a wave offering before Yahweh, with the two lambs. They shall be holy to Yahweh for the priest. **21 You shall make proclamation on the same day that it is a holy convocation to you**. You shall do no regular work. This is a statute forever in all your dwellings throughout your generations.

22 "When you reap the harvest of your land, you shall not wholly reap into the corners of your field, **neither shall you gather the gleanings of your harvest**. You shall leave them for the poor and for the foreigner. I am Yahweh your God.'"

Rom 14:5 One man esteems one day as more important. Another **esteems every day alike**. Let **each man be fully assured in his own mind**. **6** He who **observes the day, observes it to the Lord**; and he who does not observe the day, to the Lord he does not observe it. **He who eats, eats to the Lord**, for he gives God thanks. He who doesn't eat, **to the Lord he doesn't eat**, and gives God thanks.

NOTE: Paul sees opportunity in the observance of days, but also freedom to treat all days alike. Are the "two loaves of bread" -- an offering to Yahweh on a feast day -- representing these two approaches? As in the previous pairing, again Paul looks beyond the mechanics of the decision to the matter of intent: whatever you individually decide, if you do it "to the Lord" it becomes your offering of thanks to God.

Lev 23:23 Yahweh spoke to Moses, saying, **24** "Speak <u>to the children of Israel</u>, saying, 'In the seventh month, on the first day of the month, there shall be a solemn rest for you, a memorial of blowing of trumpets, a holy convocation. **25** You shall do no regular work. You shall offer an offering made by fire to Yahweh.'"

26 Yahweh spoke to Moses, saying, **27** "However on the tenth day of this seventh month is the **day of atonement**. It shall be a holy convocation to you. You shall afflict yourselves and you shall offer an offering made by fire to Yahweh. **28** You shall do no kind of work in that same day, for it is a day of atonement, <u>to make atonement for you before Yahweh your God</u>. **29** For whoever it is who shall not deny himself in that same day shall be cut off from his people. **30 Whoever does any kind of work in that same day, I will destroy that person from among his people**. **31** You shall do no kind of work: it is <u>a statute forever throughout your generations in all your dwellings</u>. **32** It shall be a Sabbath of solemn rest for you, and you shall deny yourselves. In the ninth day of the month at evening, from evening to evening, you shall keep your Sabbath."

Rom 14:7 For <u>**none of us lives to himself,**</u> and none dies to himself. **8 For if we live, we live to the Lord. Or if we die, we die to the Lord**. If therefore we live or die, we are the Lord's. **9** For to this end <u>**Christ died, rose, and lived again, that he might be Lord of both the dead and the living**</u>.

10 But you, why do you judge your brother? Or you again, why do you despise your brother? For **we will all stand before the judgment seat of Christ**. **11** For it is written, "'<u>**As I live,**'</u> says the Lord, '<u>**to me every knee will bow**</u>. Every tongue will confess to God.'" **12** So then each one of us will give account of himself to God.

NOTE: The second echo between Romans 14:8 and the "day of atonement" is related to Jewish understanding that whatever God decides on Rosh Hashana about whether a person is to live or die during the coming year, that decision is *sealed* on Yom Kippur, the day of atonement. Regarding the echo of "judgement seat of Christ" in Romans 14:10, the judgement of God is intricately connected with Yom Kippur.

Lev 23:33 Yahweh spoke to Moses, saying, **34** "Speak to the children of Israel, and say, 'On the fifteenth day of this seventh month is the feast of booths for seven days to Yahweh. **35** On the first day shall be a holy convocation. **You shall do no regular work**. **36** Seven days you shall offer an offering made by fire to Yahweh. On the eighth day shall be a holy convocation to you. You shall offer an offering made by fire to Yahweh. It is a solemn assembly; you shall do no regular work.

37 "'These are the appointed **feasts** of Yahweh which you shall proclaim to be holy convocations, to offer an offering made by fire to Yahweh, a burnt offering, a meal offering, a sacrifice, and drink offerings, each on its own day— **38** in addition to the Sabbaths of Yahweh, and in addition to your gifts, and in addition to all your vows, and in addition to all your free will offerings, which you give to Yahweh.

39 "'So on the fifteenth day of the seventh month, when you have gathered in the fruits of the land, you shall keep the feast of Yahweh seven days; on the first day shall be a solemn rest, and on the eighth day shall be a solemn rest. **40** You shall take on the first day the fruit of majestic trees, branches of palm trees, and boughs of thick trees, and willows of the brook; and you shall rejoice before Yahweh your God seven days. **41** You shall keep it as a feast to Yahweh seven days in the year. It is a statute forever throughout your generations. You shall keep it in the seventh month. **42** You shall dwell in temporary shelters for seven days. All who are native-born in Israel shall dwell in temporary shelters, **43** that your generations may know that I made the children of Israel to dwell in temporary shelters when I brought them out of the land of Egypt. I am Yahweh your God.'" **44** So Moses declared to the children of Israel the **appointed feasts** of Yahweh.

Rom 14:13 Therefore let's not judge one another anymore, but judge this rather, that **no man put a stumbling block in his brother's way**, or an occasion for falling. **14** I know and am persuaded in the Lord Jesus that nothing is unclean of itself; except that to him who considers anything to be unclean, to him it is unclean. **15** **Yet if because of food your brother is grieved**, you walk no longer in love. Don't destroy with your food him for whom Christ died. **16** Then don't let your good be slandered, **17** for God's Kingdom is not eating and drinking, but righteousness, peace, and joy in the Holy Spirit. **18** For he who serves Christ in these things is acceptable to God and approved by men. **19** So then, let's **follow after things which make for peace, and things by which we may build one another up**.

NOTE: The three Leviticus phrases that are underlined-but-not-bolded, echo in Romans: righteousness, peace and joy in the Holy Spirit.

Leviticus 24	Romans 14:20

Lev 24:1 Yahweh spoke to Moses, saying, **2** "<u>**Command the children of Israel, that they bring**</u> to you pure olive oil beaten for the light, to cause a lamp to burn continually. **3** Outside of the veil of the Testimony, in the Tent of Meeting, Aaron shall keep it in order from evening to morning before Yahweh continually. It shall be a statute forever throughout your generations. **4** He shall keep in order the lamps on the pure gold lamp stand before Yahweh continually.

5 "<u>**You shall take fine flour and bake twelve cakes**</u> of it: two tenths of an ephah shall be in one cake.

Rom 14:20 <u>**Don't overthrow God's work**</u> for food's sake. All things indeed are clean; however, it is evil for that man who creates a stumbling block by eating. **21** <u>**It is good to not eat meat, drink wine**</u>, nor do anything by which your brother stumbles, is offended, or is made weak.

Lev 24:6 You shall set them in two rows, six on a row, on the pure **gold** table before Yahweh. **7** You shall put pure frankincense on each row, that it may be to the bread for a memorial, even an offering made by fire to Yahweh. **8** Every Sabbath day he shall set it in order before Yahweh continually. It is an everlasting covenant on the behalf of the children of Israel. **9** It shall be for Aaron and his sons. They shall eat it in a holy place; <u>**for it is most holy to him of the offerings of Yahweh**</u> made by fire by a perpetual statute."

Rom 14:22 Do you have **faith**? Have it to yourself before God. Happy is he who doesn't judge himself in that which he approves. **23** But he who doubts is condemned if he eats, because it isn't of faith; and <u>**whatever is not of faith is sin**</u>.

NOTE: The first echo of this pairing is proposed based on 1 Peter 1:7. The final echo speaks very personally to the individual, including that very individual in the determination of holiness or sin.

Leviticus 24:10	Romans 15

Lev 24:10 The son of an Israelite woman, whose father was an Egyptian, went out among the children of Israel; and the son of the Israelite woman and a **man of Israel** <u>strove together</u> in the camp. **11** The <u>son of the Israelite woman blasphemed the Name</u> and cursed; and they brought him to Moses. His mother's name was Shelomith, the daughter of Dibri, of the tribe of Dan. **12** They put him in custody until Yahweh's will should be declared to them.

13 Yahweh spoke to Moses, saying, **14** "Bring him who cursed out of the camp; and let all who heard him lay their hands on his head, and let all the congregation stone him. **15** You shall speak to the children of Israel, saying, 'Whoever curses his God shall bear his sin. **16** **He who blasphemes Yahweh's name, he shall surely be put to death**. All the congregation shall certainly stone him. The foreigner as well as the native-born shall be put to death when he blasphemes the Name.

Rom 15:1 Now we **who are strong** <u>ought to bear</u> the <u>weaknesses of the weak</u>, and not to please ourselves. **2** Let each one of us please his neighbor for that which is good, to be building him up. **3** For even Christ didn't please himself. But, as it is written, "**The reproaches of those who reproached You fell on me**."

NOTE: It is not completely clear from the echoes how Paul views the outcome of the story in Leviticus. Perhaps the same advice he gives to the church in Rome would have been useful in the Leviticus story as well.

Lev 24:17 "'He who strikes any man mortally shall surely be put to death. **18** He who strikes an animal mortally shall make it good, life for life. **19** If anyone injures his neighbor, it shall be done to him as he has done: **20** fracture for fracture, eye for eye, tooth for tooth. It shall be done to him as he has injured someone. **21** He who kills an animal shall make it good; and he who kills a man shall be put to death.

Rom 15:4 For whatever things were written before were written for our learning, that through perseverance and through encouragement of the Scriptures we might have hope.

NOTE: This verse, Romans 15:4, can be seen as an echo of not just of Leviticus 24:17-21, but the entirety of the book.

Lev 24:22 You shall have **one kind of law for the foreigner as well as the native-born**; for **I am Yahweh your God**.'"	**Rom 15:5** Now the God of perseverance and of encouragement grant you to be of the same mind with one another according to Christ Jesus, **6** that with one accord you may with one mouth glorify the God and Father of our Lord Jesus Christ. **7** <u>**Therefore accept one another, even as Christ also accepted you, to the glory of God**</u>. **8** Now I say that Christ has been made a servant of the circumcision for the truth of God, that he might confirm the promises given to the fathers, **9** and **that the Gentiles might glorify God for his mercy.** As it is written, "Therefore I will give praise to you among the Gentiles and sing to your name." **10** Again he says, "Rejoice, you Gentiles, with his people." **11** Again, "Praise the Lord, all you Gentiles! Let all the peoples praise him." **12** Again, Isaiah says, "There will be the root of Jesse, he who arises to rule over the Gentiles; in him the Gentiles will hope." **13** Now may the God of hope fill you with all joy and peace in believing, that you may abound in hope in the power of the Holy Spirit.
Lev 24:23 Moses spoke to the children of Israel; and **they brought him who had cursed out of the camp** and stoned him with stones. The **children of Israel did as Yahweh commanded Moses**.	**Rom 15:14** I myself am also persuaded about you, my brothers, that you yourselves are full of goodness,**, filled with all knowledge, able also to admonish others**. **15** But I write the more boldly to you in part as reminding you, because of the grace that was given to me by God, **16** that I should be a servant of Christ Jesus to the Gentiles, serving as a priest of the Good News of God, that the offering up of the Gentiles might be made acceptable, sanctified by the Holy Spirit. **17** I have therefore my boasting in Christ Jesus in things pertaining to God. **18** For I will not dare to speak of any things except those which Christ worked through me for the **obedience of the Gentiles**, by word and deed, **19** in the power of signs and wonders, in the power of God's Spirit; so that from Jerusalem and around as far as to Illyricum, I have fully preached the Good News of Christ; **20** yes, making it my aim to preach the Good News, not where Christ was already named, that I might not build on another's foundation. **21** But, as it is written, "They will see, to whom no news of him came. Those who haven't heard will understand."

NOTE: [Emor ends.]

Leviticus 25   Romans 15:22

Lev 25:1 Yahweh said to Moses on Mount Sinai, **2** "Speak to the children of Israel, and tell them, '**When you come into the land** which I give you, then the land shall keep a Sabbath to Yahweh. **3** You shall sow your field six years, and you shall prune your vineyard six years, and gather in its fruits; **4** but in the seventh year there shall be a Sabbath of solemn rest for the **land**, a Sabbath to Yahweh. You shall not sow your field or prune your vineyard. **5** What grows of itself in your harvest you shall not reap, and you shall not gather the grapes of your undressed vine. It shall be a year of solemn rest for the land. **6** The Sabbath of the land shall be for food for you; for yourself, for your servant, for your maid, for your hired servant, **and for your stranger, who lives as a foreigner with you**. **7** For your livestock also, and for the animals that are in your land, shall all its increase be for food.

Rom 15:22 Therefore I was **hindered these many times from coming to you**, **23** but now, no longer having any **place** in these regions, and having these many years a longing to come to you, **24** **whenever I travel to Spain, I will come to you**. For I hope to see you on my journey, and to be helped on my way there by you, if first I may enjoy your company for a while.

NOTE: [Behar.]

Lev 25:8 "'You shall count off seven Sabbaths of years, seven times seven years; and there shall be to you the days of seven Sabbaths of years, even forty-nine years. 9 Then you shall sound the loud trumpet on the tenth day of the seventh month. On the Day of Atonement, **you shall sound the trumpet throughout all your land**. 10 You shall make the fiftieth year holy and proclaim liberty throughout the land <u>to all its inhabitants</u>. It shall be a jubilee to you; and each of you shall return to his own property, and each of you shall return to his family. 11 That fiftieth year shall be a jubilee to you. In it you shall not sow, neither reap that which grows of itself, nor gather from the undressed vines. **12 For it is a jubilee; it shall be holy to you. You shall eat of its increase out of the field**.

13 "'In this Year of Jubilee each of you shall return to his property. 14 "'If you sell anything to your neighbor, or buy from your neighbor, you shall not wrong one another. 15 According to the number of years after the Jubilee you shall buy from your neighbor. **<u>According to the number of years of the crops he shall sell to you</u>**. 16 According to the length of the years you shall increase its price, and according to the shortness of the years you shall diminish its price; for **he is selling the number of the crops to you**. 17 You shall not wrong one another, but you shall fear your God; for I am Yahweh your God.

18 "'Therefore you shall do my statutes and keep my ordinances and do them; and you shall dwell in the land in safety. 19 The land shall yield its fruit, <u>and you shall eat your fill, and dwell therein in safety</u>. 20 If you said, "What shall we eat the seventh year? Behold, we shall not sow, nor gather in our increase;" 21 then I will command my **<u>blessing on you in the sixth year, and it shall bear fruit for the three years</u>**. 22 You shall sow the eighth year and eat of the fruits from the old store until the ninth year. Until its fruits come in, you shall eat the old store.

Rom 15:25 **But now, I say, I am going to Jerusalem**, serving the <u>saints</u>. 26 For it has been the good pleasure of Macedonia and Achaia to **make a certain contribution for the poor among the saints who are at Jerusalem**. 27 Yes, it has been their good pleasure, **<u>and they are their debtors</u>**. For if the Gentiles have been made **partakers of their spiritual things**, they owe it to them also to serve them in material things. **28** <u>When therefore I have accomplished this, and have sealed to them this fruit</u>, I will go on by way of you to Spain. 29 I know that when I come to you, I will come in the fullness of the **<u>blessing of the Good News of Christ</u>**.

NOTE: The idea that Paul echoes the Jubilee has could well be a double meaning for Paul. First, Jubilee is a time when land is returned to its original owners, and in so doing it makes sense that the owners return to the land. Second, the Jubilee is a year that the land rests, and in which whatever harvest grows naturally is made available to those in need. Paul uses this opportunity in the letter to state the importance of Gentiles sharing material blessings with the saints in Jerusalem.

Lev 25:23 "'The land shall not be sold in perpetuity, for the land is mine; for you are strangers and live as foreigners with me. **24** In all the land of your possession you shall grant a redemption for the land.

25 "'<u>If your brother becomes poor, and sells some of his possessions, then his kinsman who is next to him shall come and redeem that which his brother has sold</u>. **26** If a man has no one to redeem it, and he becomes prosperous and finds sufficient means to redeem it, **27** then let him reckon the years since its sale and restore the surplus to the man to whom he sold it; and he shall return to his property. **28** But if he isn't able to get it back for himself, then what he has sold shall remain in the hand of him who has bought it until the Year of Jubilee. In the Jubilee it shall be released, and he shall return to his property.

29 "'If a man sells a dwelling house in a walled city, then he may redeem it within a whole year after it has been sold. For a full year he shall have the right of redemption. **30** If it isn't redeemed within the space of a full year, then the house that is in the walled city shall be made sure in perpetuity to him who bought it, throughout his generations. It shall not be released in the Jubilee. **31** But the houses of the villages which have no wall around them shall be accounted for with the fields of the country: they may be redeemed, and they shall be released in the Jubilee. **32** "'**Nevertheless, in the cities of the Levites, the Levites may redeem the houses In the cities of their possession at any time**. **33** The Levites may redeem the house that was sold, and the city of his possession, and it shall be released in the Jubilee; for the houses of the cities of the Levites are their possession among the children of Israel. **34** But the field of the pasture lands of their cities may not be sold, for it is their perpetual possession.

Rom 15:30 Now <u>I beg you, brothers</u>, by our Lord Jesus Christ and by the love of the Spirit, **that you strive together with me in your prayers** to God for me,

NOTE: Paul's language of "to beg" seems odd, but it does fit with the echo of a brother being redeemed by another brother. Indeed, it was Ruth that entreated Boaz in a powerful and personal way. The immediate desired "striving together" with Paul in prayer is echoed in the fact that the redemption of the houses of the Levites did not need to wait for the Jubilee but can happen at any time.

Lev 25:35 "'If your brother has become poor and his hand can't support himself among you, then you shall uphold him. He shall live with you like an alien and a temporary resident. **36** Take no interest from him or profit; but fear your God, that your brother may live among you. **37** You shall not lend him your money at interest, nor give him your food for profit. **38** I am Yahweh your God, who brought you out of the land of Egypt, **to give you the land of Canaan**, and to be your God.

39 "'If your brother has grown poor among you, and sells himself to you, you shall not make him to serve as a slave. **40** As a hired servant, and as a temporary resident, he shall be with you; he shall serve with you until the Year of Jubilee. **41** Then he shall go out from you, he and his children with him, and shall return to his own family, and to the possession of his fathers. **42** <u>For they are my servants, whom I brought out of the land of Egypt</u>. They shall not be sold as slaves. **43** You shall not rule over him with harshness but shall fear your God. **44** "'As for your male and your female slaves, whom you may have from the nations that are around you, from them you may buy male and female slaves. **45** Moreover, of the children of the aliens who live among you, of them you may buy, and of their families who are with you, which they have conceived in your land; and they will be your property. **46** You may make them an inheritance for your children after you, to hold for a possession; of them you may take your slaves forever, **but over your brothers the children of Israel you shall not rule, one over another, with harshness**.

Rom 15:31 that I may be delivered from **those who are disobedient in Judea**, and that <u>my service which I have for Jerusalem</u> may be **acceptable to the saints**,

NOTE: Paul's phrase "my service which I have for Jerusalem" may have something to do with preparing Jerusalem for the great coming Exodus of the end times (Jeremiah 16:14-15), and that Jerusalem will be ready for the "mountain of the house of the Lord will be established…and all the nations will stream to it." (Isaiah 2:2).

Lev 25:47 "'If an alien or temporary resident with you becomes rich, and your brother beside him has grown poor, and sells himself to the alien or temporary resident with you, or to a member of the stranger's family, **48** after he is sold he may be redeemed. One of his brothers may redeem him; **49** or his uncle, or his uncle's son, may redeem him, or any who is a close relative to him of his family may redeem him; or if he has grown rich, he may redeem himself. **50** He shall reckon with him who bought him from the year that he sold himself to him to the Year of Jubilee. The price of his sale shall be according to the number of years; he shall be with him according to the time of a hired servant. **51** If there are yet many years, according to them he shall give back the price of his redemption out of the money that he was bought for. **52** If there remain but a few years to the year of jubilee, then he shall reckon with him; according to his years of service he shall give back the price of his redemption. **53** As a servant hired year by year shall he be with him. He shall not rule with harshness over him in your sight. **54 If he isn't redeemed by these means, then he shall be released in the Year of Jubilee**: he and his children with him. **55** For to me the children of Israel are servants; they are my servants whom I brought out of the land of Egypt. I am Yahweh your God.

Leviticus 26

26:1 "'You shall make for yourselves no idols, and you shall not raise up a carved image or a pillar, and you shall not place any figured stone in your land, to bow down to it; for I am Yahweh your God. **2** You shall keep my **Sabbaths** and have reverence for my sanctuary. I am Yahweh.

NOTE: [Behar ends.]

Rom 15:32 that I may come **to you in joy through the will of God, and together** with you,

find **rest**.

Leviticus 26:3   Rom. 15:33

Lev 26:3 "'If you walk in my statutes and keep my commandments, and do them, **4** then I will give you your rains in their season, and the land shall yield its increase, and the trees of the field shall yield their fruit. **5** Your threshing shall continue until the vintage, and the vintage shall continue until the sowing time. You shall eat your bread to the full, and dwell in your land safely. **6** "'**I will give peace in the land**, and you shall lie down, and no one will make you afraid. I will remove evil animals out of the land, neither shall the sword go through your land. **7** You shall chase your enemies, and they shall fall before you by the sword. **8** Five of you shall chase a hundred, and a hundred of you shall chase ten thousand; and your enemies shall fall before you by the sword. **9** "'I will have respect for you, make you fruitful, multiply you, and will establish my covenant with you. **10** You shall eat old supplies long kept, and you shall move out the old because of the new. **11** I will set my tent among you, and my soul won't abhor you. **12** I will walk among you, and will be your God, and you will be my people. **13** I am Yahweh your God, who brought you out of the land of Egypt, that you should not be their slaves. I have broken the bars of your yoke and made you walk upright.

Rom 15:33 Now the **God of peace** be with you all. Amen.

NOTE: [Bechukotai.] Paul now moves quickly and writes one verse to the church in Rome that echoes, in multiple ways, the promises and warnings given to Israel in Leviticus 26.

Lev 26:14 "'But if you will not listen to me, and will not do all these commandments, **15** and if you shall reject my statutes, and if your soul abhors my ordinances, so that you will not do all my commandments, but break my covenant, **16** I also will do this to you: I will appoint terror over you, even consumption and fever, that shall consume the eyes, and make the soul to pine away. You will sow your seed in vain, for your enemies will eat it. **17** I will set my face against you, and you will be struck before your enemies. Those who hate you will rule over you; and you will flee when no one pursues you.

Rom 15:33 Now the God of peace be with you all. Amen.

(repeated)

NOTE: Paul now moves quickly and writes one verse to the church in Rome that echoes, in multiple ways, the promises and warnings given to Israel in Leviticus 26.

Lev 26:18 "'If you in spite of these things will not listen to me, then I will chastise you seven times more for your sins. **19** I will break the pride of your power, and I will make your sky like iron, and your soil like bronze. **20** Your strength will be spent in vain; for your land won't yield its increase, neither will the trees of the land yield their fruit. **21** "'If you walk contrary to me, and won't listen to me, then I will bring seven times more plagues on you according to your sins. **22** I will send the wild animals among you, which will rob you of your children, destroy your livestock, and make you few in number. Your roads will become desolate. **23** "'If by these things you won't be turned back to me, but will walk contrary to me, **24** then I will also walk contrary to you; and I will strike you, even I, seven times for your sins. **25** I will bring a sword upon you that will execute the vengeance of the covenant. You will be gathered together within your cities, and I will send the pestilence among you. You will be delivered into the hand of the enemy. **26** When I break your staff of bread, ten women shall bake your bread in one oven, and they shall deliver your bread again by weight. You will eat and not be satisfied. **27** "'If you in spite of this won't listen to me, but walk contrary to me, **28** then I will walk contrary to you in wrath. I also will chastise you seven times for your sins. **29** You will eat the flesh of your sons, and you will eat the flesh of your daughters. **30** I will destroy your high places, and cut down your incense altars, and cast your dead bodies upon the bodies of your idols; and my soul will abhor you. **31** I will lay your cities waste and will bring your sanctuaries to desolation. I will not take delight in the sweet fragrance of your offerings. **32** I will bring the land into desolation, and your enemies who dwell in it will be astonished at it. **33** I will scatter you among the nations, and I will draw out the sword after you. Your land will be a desolation, and your cities shall be a waste.

34 Then the land will enjoy its Sabbaths as long as it lies desolate and you are in your enemies' land. Even then the land will rest and enjoy its Sabbaths. **35** As long as it lies desolate it shall have rest, even the rest which it didn't have in your Sabbaths when you lived on it. **36** "'As for those of you who are left, I will send a faintness into their hearts in the lands of their enemies. The sound of a driven leaf will put them to flight; and they shall flee, as one flees from the sword, and they shall fall when no one pursues. **37** They shall stumble over one another, as it were before the sword, when no one pursues. You shall have no power to stand before your enemies. **38** You shall perish among the nations, and the land of your enemies shall eat you up. **39** Those of you who are left shall pine away in their iniquity in your enemies' lands; and also in the iniquities of their fathers they shall pine away with them.

Rom 15:33 Now the God of **peace be with you** all. Amen.

(repeated)

NOTE: Paul now moves quickly and writes one verse to the church in Rome that echoes, in multiple ways, the promises and warnings given to Israel in Leviticus 26.

Lev 26:40 "'If they confess their iniquity and the iniquity of their fathers, in their trespass which they trespassed against me; and also that because they walked contrary to me, **41** I also walked contrary to them, and brought them into the land of their enemies; if then their uncircumcised heart is humbled, and they then accept the punishment of their iniquity, **42** then I will remember my covenant with Jacob, my covenant with Isaac, and also my covenant with Abraham; and I will remember the land. **43** The land also will be left by them and will enjoy its **Sabbaths** while it lies desolate without them; and they will accept the punishment of their iniquity because they rejected my ordinances, and their soul abhorred my statutes. **44** Yet for all that, when they are in the land of their enemies, I will not reject them, neither will I abhor them, to destroy them utterly and to break my covenant with them; for I am Yahweh their God. **45** <u>But I will for their sake remember the covenant of their ancestors</u>, whom I brought out of the land of Egypt in the sight of the nations, that I might be their God. I am Yahweh.'"

46 These are the statutes, ordinances, and laws, which Yahweh made between him and the children of Israel in Mount Sinai by Moses.

Rom 15:33
Now the God of **peace** <u>be</u> <u>with you all</u>.
Amen.

(repeated)

NOTE: The word "Sabbaths" echoes "peace." The phrase "But I will for their sake remember the covenant of their ancestors" echoes "be with you all" since God is promising not to leave them in exile. The last verse, Leviticus 26:46 is a summary statement that echoes the word "Amen".

Leviticus 27	Romans 16

Lev 27:1 Yahweh spoke to Moses, saying, **2** "Speak to the children of Israel, and say to them, 'When a man makes a vow, the persons shall be for Yahweh by your valuation. **3** Your valuation of a male from twenty years old to sixty years old shall be fifty shekels of silver, according to the shekel of the sanctuary. **4** If **she is a female**, then **your valuation shall be thirty shekels**. **5** If the person is from five years old to twenty years old, then your valuation shall be for a male twenty shekels, and for a female ten shekels. **6** If the person is from a month old to five years old, then your valuation shall be for a male five shekels of silver, and for a female your valuation shall be three shekels of silver. **7** If the person is from sixty years old and upward; if he is a male, then your valuation shall be fifteen shekels, and for a female ten shekels. **8** But if he is poorer than your valuation, then he shall be set before the priest, and the priest shall assign him a value. **The priest shall assign a value according to his ability to pay**.

9 "'If it is an animal of which men offer an offering to Yahweh, all that any man gives of such to Yahweh becomes holy. **10** He shall not alter it, nor exchange it, a good for a bad, or a bad for a good. If he shall at all exchange animal for animal, then both it and that for which it is exchanged shall be holy. **11** If it is any unclean animal, of which they do not offer as an offering to Yahweh, then he shall set the animal before the priest; **12** and the priest shall evaluate it, whether it is good or bad. As the priest evaluates it, so it shall be**. **13** But if he will indeed redeem it, then he shall add the fifth part of it to its valuation.

Rom 16:1 I commend to you **Phoebe, our sister**, who is a servant of the assembly that is at Cenchreae, **2a that you receive her in the Lord in a way worthy of the saints**, and that **you assist her in whatever matter she may need from you**, for she herself also **has been a helper of many**,

NOTE: The above connection of "30 shekels" for "Phoebe, our sister" finds its echo in the Romans 16:1-15. Starting with "Phoebe" in verse one and ending with "Olympas" in verse 15 are exactly twenty-six proper names, along with four specific unnamed persons as follows: "me, myself" (being Paul), "his mother and mine," and "his sister", bringing the listed names to exactly 30 specific persons. While this might on its own be considered a coincidence, similar, precise numerical echoes have been found to exist in most of Paul's other epistles, often in the latter sections. Paul appears to write with precision even in the smallest of details. That practice ultimately magnifies God, because it shows us how much Paul's appreciated the precision of the inspired Hebrew scriptures.

Lev 27:14 "'When a man **dedicates his house** to be holy to Yahweh, then the priest shall evaluate it, whether it is good or bad. As the priest evaluates it, so shall it stand. **15** If he who dedicates it will redeem his house, then he shall add the fifth part of the money of your valuation to it, and it shall be his.

16 "'If a man dedicates to Yahweh part of the field of his possession, then your valuation shall be according to the seed for it. The sowing of a homer of **barley** shall be valued at fifty shekels of silver. **17** If he dedicates his **field** from the Year of Jubilee, according to your valuation it shall stand. **18 But if he dedicates his field after the Jubilee,** then the priest shall reckon to him the money according to the years that remain to the Year of Jubilee; and an abatement shall be made from your valuation. **19** If he who dedicated the field will indeed redeem it, then he shall add the fifth part of the money of your valuation to it, and it shall remain his. **20** If he will not redeem the field, or if he has sold the field to another man, it shall not be redeemed anymore; **21** but the **field**, when it goes out in the Jubilee, shall be holy to Yahweh, as a devoted field. It shall be owned by the priests. **22** "'If he dedicates a field to Yahweh which he has bought, which is not of the field of his possession, **23** then the priest shall reckon to him the worth of your valuation up to the Year of Jubilee; and he shall give your valuation on that day, as a **holy thing to Yahweh**. **24** In the Year of Jubilee the field shall return to him from whom it was bought, even to him to whom the possession of the land belongs. **25** All your valuations shall be according to the shekel of the sanctuary: twenty gerahs to the shekel.

26 "'However the firstborn among animals, which belongs to Yahweh as a firstborn, no man may dedicate, whether an ox or a sheep. It is Yahweh's.

Rom 16:2b and of me myself. **3** Greet Prisca and Aquila, my fellow workers in Christ Jesus, **4** who risked their own necks for my life, to whom not only I give thanks, but also all the assemblies of the Gentiles. **5** **Greet the assembly that is in their house**. Greet Epaenetus, my beloved, who is the **first fruits** of Achaia to Christ. **6** Greet Mary, who **labored** much for us. **7** Greet Andronicus and Junia, my relatives and my fellow prisoners, who are notable among the apostles, **who were also in Christ before me**. **8** Greet Ampliatus, my beloved in the Lord. **9** Greet Urbanus, our fellow worker in Christ, and Stachys, my beloved. **10** Greet Apelles, the approved in Christ. Greet those who are of the household of Aristobulus. **11** Greet Herodion, my kinsman. Greet them of the household of Narcissus, who are in the Lord. **12** Greet Tryphaena and Tryphosa, who labor in the Lord. Greet Persis, the beloved, who **labored** much in the Lord. **13** Greet Rufus, the chosen in the Lord, and his mother and mine. **14** Greet Asyncritus, Phlegon, Hermes, Patrobas, Hermas, and the brothers who are with them. **15** Greet Philologus and Julia, Nereus and his sister, and Olympas, and all the saints who are with them. **16** Greet one another with a **holy kiss.** The assemblies of Christ greet you.

NOTE: The echo of "but if he dedicates a field after the Jubilee" with "who were in Christ before me" is suggested because Paul is giving honor to those persons who "labored in the field" before he came into the picture and began to work the field himself. This parallels the idea that a field worked by one owner may be bought by another to be worked, but ultimately the field returns to its original owner.

Lev 27:27 If it is an **unclean** animal, then he shall buy it back according to your valuation and shall add to it the fifth part of it; or if it isn't redeemed, **then it shall be sold according to your valuation**.

28 "'Notwithstanding, no devoted thing that a man devotes to Yahweh of all that he has, whether of man or animal, or of the field of his possession, shall be sold or redeemed. **Every devoted thing is most holy to Yahweh**. 29 "'No one **devoted to destruction**, who shall be devoted from among men, shall be ransomed. He shall surely be put to death.

Rom 16:17 Now I beg you, brothers, look out for those who are **causing the divisions and occasions of stumbling**, contrary to the doctrine which you learned, and turn away from them. 18 **For those who are such don't serve our Lord Jesus Christ, but their own belly**; and by their smooth and flattering speech they deceive the hearts of the innocent.

19 For your obedience has become known to all. I rejoice therefore over you. But I desire to have you **wise in that which is good, but innocent in that which is evil**. 20 And the God of peace will quickly crush **Satan** under your feet. The grace of our Lord Jesus Christ be with you.

Lev 27:30 "'All the tithe of the land, whether of the seed of the land or of the fruit of the trees, is Yahweh's. It is holy to Yahweh. **31** If a man redeems anything of his <u>tithe</u>, he shall add a fifth part to it. **32** All the tithe of the herds or the flocks, whatever passes under the rod, **the tenth shall be holy to Yahweh**. **33** He shall not examine whether it is good or bad, neither shall he exchange it. If he exchanges it at all, then both it and that for which it is exchanged shall be holy. It shall not be redeemed.'"

Rom 16:21 <u>Timothy</u>, my fellow worker, greets you, as do <u>Lucius</u>, <u>Jason</u>, and <u>Sosipater</u>, my relatives. **22** I, <u>Tertius</u>, who write the letter, greet you in the Lord. **23** <u>Gaius</u>, my host and host of the whole assembly, greets you. <u>Erastus, the treasurer of the city</u>, greets you, as does <u>Quartus, the brother</u>. **24** The grace of our Lord **Jesus Christ** be with you all! Amen.

NOTE: Romans 16:21-24 lists eight persons. Paul, as the author is not listed but is clearly part of the group. And "Jesus Christ," is specifically listed in Rom. 16:24, and is present with them in Spirit (Matthew 18:20). The grand total is ten persons, which matches the "tithe" listed in Leviticus 27:31. Given that Jesus Christ is listed tenth, an echo is suggested between "Jesus Christ" and "the tenth shall be holy to Yahweh," possibly an opportunity taken by Paul to simply honor our Lord and Savior yet again.

Lev 27:34 <u>These</u> are the **commandments which Yahweh commanded** Moses **for the children of Israel** on **Mount Sinai**.

Rom 16:25 Now to him who is able to establish you according to my **Good News and the preaching of Jesus Christ**, according to the revelation of the mystery which has been kept secret through long ages, **26** but now is revealed, and by the Scriptures of the prophets, **according to the commandment of the eternal God**, is made known for obedience of faith **to all the nations**; **27** to the only wise God, through Jesus Christ, to whom be the **glory** forever! Amen.

NOTE: [Bechukotai ends.] While Leviticus concludes with the glory of the commandments given to Moses for Israel gathered at Sinai, Paul concludes with the revelation of the mystery now revealed by the commandment of God for all the nations to come to obedience of faith to God through Jesus Christ, to whom be the glory. Amen.

THE STORY OF THE ECHOES BIBLE

The discovery of the ancient connections between Paul's New Testament letters and the Old Testament books was made by John David Pitcher in 2008. He has published material on these connections under the title *The Oldest Midrash*. His discoveries were made primarily through linguistic analysis of the Septuagint in comparison with the New Testament. For more information see echoesbible.org/john-david-pitcher/.

When Bob O'Dell first learned of David's discoveries, he began to examine them carefully to determine whether the claims were true. David asserted in 2015 that six of Paul's epistles connected to major books of the Old Testament: Genesis to Hebrews, Exodus to Galatians, Leviticus to Romans, Numbers to 2 Timothy, Deuteronomy to 1 Timothy, and Joshua to Titus—discoveries made between 2008 and 2012. Once learning of the discovery, Bob devoted nine months to studying David's assertions in the first three pairings listed above, declaring David's discoveries to be valid. Bob found that, although he already considered himself skilled in "seeing Jesus in every page of the Old Testament," it nevertheless required time to begin perceiving those passages in the same light in which Paul himself had seen them. Paul saw far more, and Bob had to learn how Paul approached those texts—an approach that was both deeper and, at times, more obvious than he expected. It was as though, after many years of Bible study, Bob was reading the Scriptures again for the first time. Yet it was not that the truth itself was new, for Paul's words had not changed. Rather, the primary insight lay in the beauty and awe of how Paul conceptualized the Old Testament texts within the life of ancient Israel. The work of Christ was fully prefigured! It is no wonder that Paul would declare that all Scripture is useful for doctrine.

Over the next five years, with new eyes to perceive Paul's writings, Bob O'Dell combined linguistic analysis with thematic resonance, thereby both deepening the connections identified in David's discoveries and making additional, as yet unpublished discoveries as well. Whereas David has focused on the midrashic aspect of Paul's literary decisions within the academic realm, Bob has concentrated on the echoes between the Testaments—showing how each text further contextualizes and illuminates the other. His desire was that serious Bible students around the world might experience what he himself experienced: to be filled with awe and wonder at God, His Word, and the finished work of His Son. This has led to the formation of the Echoes Bible Foundation, a U.S. based 501(c)3 organization whose mission is to disseminate these insights both in print and online. Bob and David remain close friends.

The World English Bible (WEB) is used for the text due to its non-copyright status. The Echoes Bible Foundation considers the decision by eBible.org to publish a non-copyrighted modern English version of the Bible based on the non-copyrighted *New American Standard 1901*, to be a magnificent gift to the modern world.

For more on the Echoes Bible see echoesbible.org or echoesbible.com.

NOTES

NOTES

NOTES

NOTES

NOTES

NOTES

NOTES

NOTES

NOTES

NOTES